Digital Guest Experience

Tools to help hotels to manage and optimize the digital guest experience

Björn Radde

1st edition

© 2017 Björn Radde

Publisher: tredition GmbH, Hamburg, Germany

ISBN Paperback: 978-3-7323-9337-4
ISBN e-Book: 978-3-7323-9338-1

„There is nothing in the world that does not change, nothing remains eternally the way it once was.“

Zhuangz Zhou (369 - 286 BC)

Table of contents

Foreword

In deciding to write a book about the use of innovative technologies in the hotel industry, two factors were crucial:

Firstly that, with their huge budgets, Online Travel Agencies (OTAs) like Booking.com, Expedia, Agoda, Orbitz and HRS dominate online distribution and, linked to this, the realization that hotels now have very little chance in terms of direct online sales. With a few exceptions, hotels rely on the OTA sales channel. However, investments already made in online marketing measures will change radically with the appearance of voice-controlled systems such as Amazon Echo and Google Home. This became apparent to me after visiting the Google Travel Executive Forum at Google's EMEA headquarter in Dublin (Ireland), where it was impressively shown how advanced voice-controlled applications already are, and what future hotel bookings will look like. Even large companies like Booking.com and Expedia will find it increasingly challenging to influence how they appear in the relevant set in a voice-controlled search. Autonomous integration into voice assistant systems will be difficult for individual hotels and hotel chains. To this extent, hotel businesses and hotel groups should consider moving their marketing budget towards digital guest experience tools in order to, firstly, increase their revenue in the hotel and, secondly, to improve guest loyalty for future bookings.

The second factor that led to the writing of this book was that the hotel sector has enjoyed increasing occupancy over recent years.

1

This means that many hotels no longer have a problem of distribution – occupancy rates are good. Revenues can no longer be increased by selling more beds, but only by opening new hotels or putting rates up. It is scarcely realized that guests who are already in the hotel can also be monetarized. Hotels invest little in existing technological tools to optimize the guest experience in the hotel in order to increase revenues during the guest's stay and improve revenue per guest. The term ARPU (Average Revenue Per User), familiar in other sectors, is rarely used in the hotel industry, but it will probably become more significant over the coming years. To this extent, digital guest experience tools will become far more important.

Meanwhile, even the traditionalists in the sector seem to have caught on that digitalization in the hotel industry is not merely a trend, but rather a key change driver for an entire sector. Nonetheless, there is still some uncertainty when it comes to judging the speed of change and the question as to how the hotel operation itself should address this development.

I am convinced that only hotel groups and individual hotels that continue to invest in innovative technologies such as digital guest experience tools will survive the coming years. The hospitality sector is still not sufficiently innovative and is not entirely alive to this future digitalization trend. In this context, technologically innovative guest experience tools are an investment area within the digital hotel value creation chain that the hotel sector urgently needs to look at and use.

2

Only a few hotels and hotel chains understand the technological imperative and are using so-called pilots to roll out digital tools for their guests in the hotel (on-property). The momentum of on-property solutions is set to accelerate and it is heading in only one direction. In the near future, the entire hotel will be digitalized.

Finally, I wish to point out that the contents of this book represent my own opinion. They do not necessarily reflect the views of my employer or of companies known to me personally. I have received no reimbursement of any type, either from my employer or from any company referred to as an example in the book, for mentioning them in the sections concerned.

Königstein im Taunus (Germany), February 2017

Björn Radde

Acknowledgment

Even though this book was written in my spare time, I would like to thank Richard Wiegmann (Managing Director & Chief Commercial Officer of Sabre Hospitality Solutions EMEA) for his trust and support during my work at Trust International and Sabre Hospitality. Without the opportunity to participate in congresses, trade fairs and events as well as the opportunity to meet with international hoteliers to discuss their digital challenges, this book would hardly have been possible.

Special thanks go to Olaf Slater (Director International Strategy & Innovation at Sabre Hospitality Solutions EMEA), with whom I have always been able to discuss constructively the new technologies and their application possibilities in the hotel industry. Olaf Slater has also accompanied me during the compilation of this book and provided me regularly with new information, contributed innovative ideas, and gave me valuable insights from the hotel technology. He has therefore played an important role in writing this book.

In this list Alex Alt (President of Sabre Hospitality Solutions) cannot be missing, who has always listened to my ideas whenever I met him.

I would also like to thank Dirk Führer (former Chief Executive Officer of Worldhotels and co-founder of Okanda), who has always been a valuable discussion partner during the book making process and has opened my eyes to the hotel industry.

I would like to thank Jens Klemann (Managing Partner of Strateco) for the thought exchange of customer relationship management in the hotel industry. I would also like to thank Peter Agel (Vice President Technology & Thinktank at the Travel Industry Club) for the always interesting exchange of expertise.

However, I am deeply grateful to my wife, Sarah, for bearing my passion for the subject of digitization and making this book possible at all. She has always supported me, believed in me, gave me the necessary space for writing, and frequently asked critical questions to rework individual passages or whole chapters. I would also like to thank my parents and my sisters.

A warm thank you goes to all proofreaders as well as to all who have supported me with this book and I have not mentioned here personally. This includes all team members of Sabre's product management team located in Frankfurt (Germany), who have answered my technical questions and have read my unfinished drafts. I would also like to thank my colleagues at the Digital Experience unit based in Washington D.C. in the United States.

My last thanks go to all the critics who have wondered why I am writing a book at all, discarding the topic for foolish visions of the future, and holding time. This criticism was another motivator to actually be finished.

I would like to dedicate this book to my children!

Chapter 1

Introduction

1 Introduction

Online distribution is increasingly important for the hotel industry in Europe.[1] On average, over half of all hotel rooms in Europe are now booked online and this market share is growing rapidly.[2] At the same time, hotels are increasingly dependent on a few, large market participants.[3] The Online Travel Agencies (OTA) such as Booking.com, Expedia, Agoda, Orbitz and HRS dominate online marketing with huge budgets.[4] The role of the OTAs is no longer that of intermediary, but that of gatekeeper.

The power of hotel metasearch engines such as Trivago and Kayak has also increased substantially.[5] Google, too, is now involved in this area. In November 2015 Google abandoned its Hotel Finder as a standalone application and integrated the function into its normal search results. This makes Google's digital hotel marketing status

---

[1]   See Warnecke, Tobias: "Hotelmarkt Deutschland 2016", 2016, P. 254
[2]   See Statista: "Online Reisebuchungen"
      https://dc.statista.com/outlook/262/137/online-
      reisebuchungen/deutschland#, 2015 and Kauer-Berk, Oliver:
      "Größter Schwachpunkt ist fehlende Vergleichbarkeit", 2016,
      https://www.welt.de/reise/article152553504/Groesster-
      Schwachpunkt-ist-fehlende-Vergleichbarkeit.html
[3]   See Kwidzinski, Raphaela: "Die großen Portale haben ihre Tücken"
      in: Allgemeine Hotel- und Gastronomie-Zeitung, No. 50, 2012, P. 8
[4]   See May, Kevin: "Expedia spent $2.8 billion on marketing in 2014",
      2014, https://www.tnooz.com/article/expedia-marketing-technology-
      spend-2014/
[5]   See Grzona, Lukas: "Immer den günstigsten Hotelpreis finden",
      2016, https://www.netzsieger.de/k/hotelsuchmaschinen

even more significant. Particularly as the organic search results for individual hotels can no longer be found in the visible area.

In this context, it is interesting that the so-called review portals such as TripAdvisor and HolidayCheck play a major role on Google, particularly with user-generated content. But the review portals have become booking portals now, too. The review portal visitor can make a booking without having to leave the portal. The booking is made in the review portal's interface.

With Google it is ironic that voice search, as a subject, has been of importance to Google for some years, and has been an established part of online searching for a long time. Even though searching by voice input using the various assistants is now pervasive, it is still often being used to avoid manual entries using a keyboard – but this might soon be changing. Even since before Google's (Siri) and Microsoft's (Cortana) voice assistants, users have been becoming increasingly accustomed to talking and asking questions using their smartphones. Up to now, the reply has appeared in a conventional search results list.

With the prevalence of physical assistants such as Amazon Echo and Google Home, users are increasingly expecting to receive replies via voice output, and not have to look at a search results list and put the information together themselves.

It is precisely this technical change, and users' expectations, that is set to change the online distribution landscape in the hotel industry for good.

As well as online booking behavior and the technical revolution of voice-controlled systems, cloud applications, mobile Internet use, social media and big data are also changing social trends.

In the hotel industry, guests' behavior is increasingly digital. Not just that hotel bookings are now made round the clock from home and most of them increasingly using mobile devices, but guests' expectations of their hotel stay have been changed by digitalization. [6] A functioning WLAN (Wi-Fi) is now almost a basic requirement. [7] Guests now also want, or even expect, digital check-in and check-out, a digital guest folder, digital delivery of newspapers, magazines and sightseeing tips, online table reservations in the hotel restaurant and online spa treatment bookings.

This presents completely new opportunities for hotels: the digital transformation of the touchpoints with their guests means that digital hotel experience tools offer the opportunity to be in permanent contact. Guests can be given the right information and offerings with great accuracy and no wastage.

Alongside the technological changes in the hotel sector, there is also currently a particularly positive situation in general in terms of financial figures. For example, the upward trend in all of the NH Hotel Group's business areas in the first three quarters of 2016 led

---

[6] See study by The Futures Company for InterContinental Hotel: "Creating 'moments of trust' The key to building successful brand relationships in the Kinship Economy", 2013, P. 11

[7] See anon.: "Was sich Gäste im Hotel am meisten wünschen", 2012, https://www.welt.de/reise/article106131007/Was-sich-Gaeste-im-Hotel-am-meisten-wuenschen.html

to a revenue increase of 6.7 percent to 1.1 billion euros, a 27.3 percent increase in EBITDA to 124.6 million euros, and a 1.8 percentage point rise in the EBITDA margin. The increase in RevPAR continued in the first three quarters (plus 6.3 percent) and is almost solely due to the growth in ADR (plus 5.2 percent).[8]

The economic situation in the German hotel industry continues to be extremely positive. According to the DEHOGA business survey, 68.6 percent of the hotels questioned between April and September 2016 rate their business outlook as good and only 5.3 percent as poor. 26.1 percent were keeping their business stable. This meant that the mood amongst hoteliers had again improved relative to the previous year. In overall terms, the outlook improved from plus 53.6 to plus 63.3 percentage points. The trend towards taking vacations in Germany has continued despite the summer weather being merely average. The vacation hotel sector grew in 2016. Urban tourism and business travel also continue to be unusually robust. As well as the positive situation in the economy as a whole, the price-quality ratio, relatively good in international terms, also resulted in growth in the German hotel sector.[9]

According to figures released by the German Federal Statistical Office, overnight stays rose by 3.0 percent to 349.7 million between January and September 2016. This is the seventh consecutive annual increase. Within this, the number of overnight stays by

---

[8]   See anon.: "NH Hotel Group verzeichnet starkes Wachstum", 2016, http://www.tophotel.de/20-news/7916-gesch%C3%A4ftszahlen-nh-hotel-group-verzeichnet-starkes-wachstum.html

[9]   See anon.: DEHOGA economic survey autumn 2016, P. 1

foreign guests rose by two percent to 62.9 million, while German stays rose by three percent to 286.8 million.[10]

Resilient European economies, the continued popularity of Mediterranean leisure destinations and Europe's importance for business travelers, should drive hotel occupancy and revenues in 2017, according to the latest PwC European Cities Hotel Forecast.[11]

Also thee U.S. hotel industry's three key performance indicators performed well in 2016, as occupancy was nearly flat (+0.1 percent to 65.5 percent), but ADR increased 3.1 percent to $123.97 and RevPAR rose 3.2 percent to $81.19 compared to 2015.[12]

The Australian hotel industry is responding to continued record international visitor growth. Through the first 11 months of the year, international arrivals to Australia increased 11.3 percent

---

[10] See anon.: German Federal Statistical Office: "Binnenhandel, Gastgewerbe, Tourismus - Ergebnisse der Monatserhebung im Tourismus", Subject-matter series 6 Series 7.1, 2016, P. 4ff.

[11] See Trunkfield, David / Mayer, Nicolas: "Standing out from the crowd: European cities hotel forecast for 2017 and 2018", 2017, http://www.pwc.com/gx/en/hospitality-leisure/assets/european-hotels-forecast-report-2017-2018-web.pdf

[12] See Higley, Jeff / Minerd, Nick: "US hotel performance for total-year 2016, Q4 2016", 2017, http://www.hotelnewsnow.com/Articles/108067/STR-US-hotel-performance-for-total-year-2016-Q4-2016

compared with the same time period in 2015, according to the Australian Bureau of Statistics.[13]

Africa is seeing a significant growth in international travelers, Hotels in the Asia Pacific region are reporting good performance for total-year 2016 and even the Mexican tourism industry experiencing its best performance ever.[14]

To summarize, it is apparent that hotels are finding it hard to compete with the online marketing power of the OTAs, and that the use of voice-controlled assistant systems such as Amazon's Alex and Google's Allo is set to disruptively change online marketing and make it even tougher for hotels to appear in potential guests' searches than has been the case up to now. To this extent, shifting investment from online marketing to digital guest experience tools could be useful to achieve better monetarization of guests during their stay.

Add to this the fact that hotels currently have high occupancy rates and good RevPar. Maintaining spending on online marketing is not recommended in this situation, either, since empty bed capacity is limited. Supported by changed guest behavior in terms of using digital devices, and changed expectations, only investing in technologically innovative guest experience tools will create the

---

[13] See anon.: "2016 Asia Pacific hotel performance", 2017, http://www.hospitalitynet.org/news/4080566.html
[14] See anon.: "Mexican tourism industry experiencing its best performance ever", 2017, http://www.tourism-review.com/mexican-tourism-sector-booming-news5324

potential to generate more revenue per guest and thus, ultimately, increase profits.

1.1 Objective

This book does not focus on underlying technicalities or detailed technical descriptions of digital guest experience tools. Care was deliberately taken to only go into important technological issues in order to provide the necessary basic understanding and to reduce the complexity of the subject. The primary focus of the book is rather to present the options for using innovative technologies in the hotel industry in order to illustrate the potential for increasing revenue, reducing costs, and improving competitiveness, guest satisfaction and loyalty.

The book also aims to provide an overview of future application scenarios for hotels in order to prepare hotel businesses and hoteliers for the unstoppable digital changes in the hotel sector.

The publication aims to be a textbook and manual that attempts to illustrate the options for deploying innovative technologies for the hotel industry. The hope is that it will particularly inspire the target group of specialists in hotels and hotel groups, i.e. eCommerce managers, eBusiness managers, digital marketing managers and marketing managers. The book also addresses the chief marketing officer and, if there is one, the chief digital officer. Hotel owners, hotel directors and business leaders (directors and CEOs) should also feel it is relevant to them, of course. But anyone interested in technology or hotels is also very welcome to read the book.

The book aims to inspire people to think, to show future developments, to probe new avenues, and to put forward specific implementation ideas. The content should not be regarded, however, as an instruction to implement all the tools immediately. The number of tools and the usefulness of implementing them will differ from hotel to hotel.

This book is not only intended to provide practical ideas, but also to be used in education and research, and to spark academic debate.

1.2 Structure

The Introduction having once more highlighted the relevance of the digital guest experience as a subject, the second chapter will indicate the main issues underlying the digital customer journey in the hotel industry and in the hotel, and explain the paradigm shift that is occurring and will occur in the pre-stay phase, and focus on the digital guest experience in the hotel. The term 'digital guest experience' as contrasted with the term 'customer journey' will be delimited and pinned down.

The third chapter will then describe digital guest experience tools in detail. For each tool, we define and describe in detail how it is used in the hotel, the challenges faced, and what return on investment it brings in terms of growing revenue, reducing costs, creating competitive advantage or improving guest satisfaction. In some cases we provide an overview of the future development of the digital guest experience tool concerned.

The book describes nine different tools, laying no claim to completeness. Developments in this sector are so dynamic that no author could record all of the technologies and deployment options in the hotel and publish an up-to-date summary. Care has been taken, however, to cover the relevant trends.

The fourth chapter then deals with the potential financial, technological, psychological, legal, strategic and operational barriers that exist or could arise when implementing digital guest experience tools. The chapter also attempts to explain ways in which these barriers may be reduced.

The book concludes with a brief conclusion and a look at the future which states that future editions will add to the list of digital guest experience tools. At the rear of the book, as well as the bibliography and list of figures, there is an index so that readers can quickly find the page they are interested in.

Great care was taken in selecting and citing the literature that supports the statements made in this book. As the subject concerned is an innovative area in the hotel industry, there is little information in the conventional secondary literature that reflects the current or, indeed, the previous research situation. Alongside academic publications we often refer to online articles and blogs. The information that was found and used has been carefully reviewed to ensure it is plausible and valid. In general, we attempted to achieve a certain balance between online and offline sources in order to underline the book's credibility and academic claims.

Chapter 2

Digital customer journey and digital guest experience

2 Digital customer journey and digital guest experience

While the subject of the customer experience is, indeed, a modern phenomenon, it has been debated for several years. For example, customer experience as an academic issue goes back to around 1982. As the construct of the customer experience, with all the behavioral science papers, would go beyond the remit of this book, the sections that follow only go into the theoretical background briefly.

There has been very little focus on customer experience in the hotel sector in past publications, even though the industry is predestined for academic research in the area of customer experience. Although here the concept has to be adapted to guest experience, which is indeed done in the definition in the next section.

As society has become digitalized, the customer experience has also been digitalized in many areas of the customer journey (particularly the on-property phase). This book aims to reflect this significance. To this extent, the content that follows always focuses on the digital aspect, and always refers to the digital guest journey and the digital guest experience.

2.1 Phases in the digital customer journey

The customer journey is based on funnel-based buying process models, the basic thinking behind which can be traced back to the AIDA model used in research into the effectiveness of advertising.[15] The AIDA model postulates that consumers pass through the stages of attention, interest, desire and action.[16] Building on the thought behind the AIDA model, funnel-based models (also known as branch purchase funnels) map a consumer's purchase decision-making process and originate in the Sequential Multistage Process Model.[17] This model shows, in simplified form, the buying process in a market compared with rival brands. The process divides up the decision-making process that a consumer goes through when purchasing a product into different, sequential stages.[18]

---

[15] See Esch, Franz-Rudolf / Brunner, Christian / Hartmann, Kerstin: "Kaufprozessorientierte Modelle der Markenführung auf dem Prüfstand: Ein Vergleich mit einem ganzheitlichen, verhaltenswissenschaftlichen Model der Markenführung", 2008, P. 147

[16] See Kroeber-Riel, Werner / Weinberg, Peter / Gröppel-Klein, Andrea: "Konsumentenverhalten", 2009, P. 633f

[17] See Esch, Franz-Rudolf / Langner, Tobias: "Branding als Grundlage zum Markenaufbau" in: Esch, Franz-Rudolf (ed.): "Moderne Markenführung", 2005, P. 573ff.

[18] See Recke, Tobias / Einhorn, Martin: "Markencontrolling bei der Dr. Ing. h.c. Porsche AG" in: Burmann, Christoph / König, Verena / Meurer, Jörg (ed.): "Identitätsbasierte Luxusmarkenführung", 2012, P. 311

A further development of funnel-based buying process models is the customer journey – their journey through the purchase decision-making process.

Synonymous with the expression 'customer journey', the expression 'consumer decision journey' is also used in the literature.[19] The concept of the customer journey divides into the phases of identifying a need (with an initial consideration set), the consumer's active evaluation, the moment of purchase and the post-purchase phase.[20]

In the hotel industry, the customer journey can be divided into three phases: the pre-stay, stay and post-stay phases. Though Figure 1 shows the customer journey in linear form, it should be regarded as a cycle, since after the hotel stay is before the hotel stay.

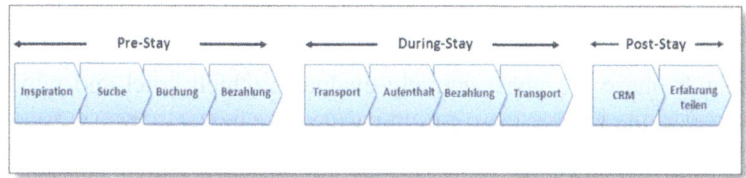

Fig. 1: "Customer journey in the hotel industry"
Source: own diagram, 2016

---

[19] See Jaffe, Joseph: "Flip the Funnel: How to Use Existing Customers to Gain New Ones", 2010, P. 53f
[20] See Court, David et al.: "The consumer decision journey", o.A., http://www.mckinsey.com/business-functions/marketing-and-sales/our-insights/the-consumer-decision-journey

The individual phases in the customer journey can, again, be subdivided into separate, sequential areas which we shall explain below.

2.1.1 Pre-stay phase

The pre-stay phase may be further subdivided into the areas inspiration, search, book and pay. Whereas the inspiration area used to be a task for catalogs and travel agencies, in the digital age it is performed by social media channels, newsletters and even small banners on websites. The guest is inspired by travel reports on blogs or by acquaintances' photos on Facebook and Instagram.[21] One click on an interesting banner takes the potential guest to an inspiring website.[22]

This behavior undoubtedly tends to be truer of leisure guests and the vacation hotel sector. Business guests usually begin by deliberately searching for a hotel in a given destination. In the search phase the guest actively evaluates which hotel and which brand might be considered for their booking decision. In the search process the guest is supported by the Google search engine. It

---

[21] See anon.: "The Hotel Customer Journey", 2015, https://www.hotelgenius.co/index.php/the-hotel-customer-journey/

[22] See Plewinski, Tina: "Amazon will Kunden mit hochwertigen Inspirationen verführen", 2016, https://www.amazon-watchblog.de/sortiment/626-amazon-hochwertige-inspirationen-verfuehren.html

should be noted, here, that more search queries are now being submitted by mobile device than using stationary computers.[23]

The guest can then make the booking itself on the hotel's website or via an OTA. The decision to book is made on the hotel's website or on the website of the relevant OTA. From a behavioral science perspective, it should be pointed out that factors at the point of sale (here, the website), such as the transparency of the booking process, price transparency, rate and room information displays, and trust-building measures (e.g. quality seals or user ratings) have a major influence on the decision.[24]

In the final step of the pre-stay phase, the booking is paid for. Even though innovative digital payment methods exist, the payment or deposit is usually made by credit card.

2.1.2 Stay phase

Compared with the pre-stay phase, digital areas are still not being widely used during the stay phase. This book aims to help increase the number of digital touchpoints for the hotel guest in the hotel.

When travelling to the hotel, guests might use their smartphone to call a cab or use a navigation app to find the hotel. In the hotel itself,

---

[23] See Kunz, Christian: "Fast 60 Prozent der Suchanfragen stammen von Mobilgeräten", 2016, https://www.seo-suedwest.de/1834-report-60-prozent-suchanfragen-mobilgeraete.html

[24] See Noël, Jean-Marc / Pohle, Jan: "Vertrauen in E-Commerce", 2005, P. 4f.

the guest's digital experience is limited to logging into the WLAN (Wi-Fi) and, at best, the hotel's own app that provides further information about the hotel. Features like digital concierge services, digital signage, indoor navigation, beacons and IoT are rare. When it comes to payment, the hotel is usually restricted to credit card or cash as the payment method. Payment options such as Apple Pay, Google Wallet, PayPal and Bitcoins have not yet properly caught on in the hotel industry.[25]

2.1.3 Post-stay phase

Once the guest leaves the hotel and sets off for home, the post-stay phase begins. The guest's experience during their hotel stay will influence their future booking behavior in terms of the hotel selected or the hotel chain or brand selected. If their experience was positive, the future booking decision may become automatic and be abbreviated. A loyalty may be generated which is expressed in the guest returning. Based on their hotel experience some guests may become so-called active loyalists, who offer their opinion on portals such as TripAdvisor and HolidayCheck , and on social networks.[26]

As this book only deals with digital guest experience tools within the digital customer journey, the remarks above only relate to hotel

---

[25] See Wolf, John: "Apple Pay Checks In to Marriott – First Hotel Company to Offer the Service to Its Guests", 2015, http://news.marriott.com/2015/03/apple-pay-checks-in-to-marriott-first-hotel-company-to-offer-the-service-to-its-guests/

[26] See Kumar, V. / Shah, Denish: "Building and sustaining profitable customer loyalty for the 21st century." in: "Journal of Retailing", 2004, Edition No. 4, P. 318f.

guests' digital touchpoints. To this extent, we need to look at the digital touchpoints within a customer touchpoint management system in greater detail. We shall do this in the next section.

2.1.4 Customer touchpoint management

Customer touchpoint management refers to the coordinating of all of the hotel's own measures that offer the guest a synchronized, trustworthy experience at any interaction point, without overlooking process efficiency. It also involves preventing guest disappointments and generating moments of enthusiasm above and beyond the base line of satisfaction.[27]

Touchpoints occur between the hotel and the guest. As moments of truth, they constitute the main decision-making basis in terms of the guest booking or not booking, or acting or not acting.[28] Throughout the booking process, the hotel stay and the post-stay phase, the main touchpoints can be identified and managed.

For example, in 2016 AccorHotels invested 230 million euros in digitalizing the entire customer journey and gaining the customer's loyalty – from inspiration, through planning and booking a trip, to

---

[27] See Schüller, Anne: "Touch. Point. Sieg. Kommunikation in Zeiten der digitalen Transformation", 2016, P. 155

[28] See Esch, Franz-Rudolf / Knörle, Christian: "Omni-Channel-Strategien durch Customer-Touchpoint-Management erfolgreich realisieren" in: Binckenbanck, Lars / Elste, Rainer (ed.): "Digitalisierung im Vertrieb – Strategien zum Einsatz neuer Technologien in Vertriebsorganisationen", 2016, P. 136

the stay itself and then a return visit using a customer loyalty scheme.[29]

2.2 Paradigm shift in the digital customer journey

As explained in the previous section, there are currently many digital touchpoints in the pre-stay phase. Hotels are able to deploy the full eDistribution repertoire here. The hotel's eCommerce Manager or a hotel chain's eCommerce department effectively divides the available budget across the different channels such as display advertising, search engine marketing (SEO and SEA), optimizing the company website, rankings in metasearch engines and commission for OTAs.

With the penetration of voice assistant systems such as Amazon Echo and Google Home, this budget allocation paradigm is set to experience a disruptive change in the coming years.

The subject of voice searching has interested Google for many years, and it has been an established online search component for some time. Even though voice searching using the various assistants is now omnipresent, it is still often being used to initiate a normal online search and to avoid manual entries using a keyboard – but this might soon be changing. And this very change is not only of concern to analysts who see a threat to Google's business model,

---

[29] See Hucho, Michael: "Alles digital? Über die Digitalisierung in Hotellerie und Gastronomie" in: "Hoga aktiv", 2016, P. 4

but it should also get online marketing managers thinking about their future role.

Automatic voice assistants and dialog systems such as Apple's Siri, Google's Allo and Microsoft's Cortana are being increasingly used.[30] Users are growing increasingly accustomed to using their smartphones to chat, ask questions and formulate tasks. The replies then generally appear in a conventional search results list.

But, particularly as these assistants become more widespread, users' expectations are increasingly changing, moving towards receiving replies by voice too, without having to look at a results list and put the information together themselves. Google is also working on providing replies to specific questions by voice and no longer showing the user long results lists.[31]

To this extent, online marketing can be expected to undergo enormous change. Traditional banners will no longer be needed, as they are not visible with voice output. The question is open as to whether hotels will be able to pay for voice-controlled recommendations as they do with pay-per-click displays. However,

[30] See Urbach, Niels / Ahlemann, Frederik: "IT-Management im Zeitalter der Digitalisierung", 2016, P. 8

[31] See Dettweiler, Marco: "Google sagt Allo zu Apple", 2016, http://www.faz.net/aktuell/technik-motor/computer-internet/neuer-messenger-ausprobiert-google-sagt-allo-zu-apple-14444681.html and Lobe, Adrian: "Allo, wer spricht denn da?", 2016, http://www.faz.net/aktuell/feuilleton/medien/neue-google-app-allo-wer-spricht-denn-da-14446431.html

it is extremely probable that it will be the OTAs, with their higher marketing spends on Google, who do this.

Since, in the future, hotels will find it increasingly difficult to play a relevant role in the digital touchpoints in the pre-stay phase, there is justification in considering a shift of budget towards digital touchpoints in the hotel (on-property). Investing in digital guest experience tools can improve revenue per guest during their hotel stay, save money and optimize processes. Findings from the customer journey (stay phase) will be used for this purpose and effectively transferred to digital guest experience tools as part of the customer touchpoint strategy.

2.3 Digital guest experience defined and classified

In the literature, customer experience refers to the entirety of all the personal impressions and interactions, across all touchpoints, that a customer has, over their lifetime, from a company and its services.[32]

Transferred to the hotel industry and enriched by the issue of digitalization, the digital guest experience is defined as follows so that it will be understood through this book:

---

[32] According to Gentile, Chiara / Spiller, Nicola / Noci, Giuliano: "How to Sustain the Customer Experience: An Overview of Experience Components that Co-create Value With the Customer" in: "European Management Journal", Issue 5, 2007, P. 397

> *The digital guest experience is the personal perception and the interaction with the digital service provided which a guest experiences while staying in the hotel.*

As the definition indicates, this book specifically assigns the digital guest experience and digital guest experience tools to the second phase (during the stay) of the customer journey, so it relates to all of the guest's direct and indirect digital touchpoints during their hotel stay.

Hotels now face the challenge of managing the digital guest experience and aligning the various customer touchpoints in the hotel in such a way that the guest has a positive experience. To put it another way, customer experience management is the creating of positive customer experiences to generate an emotional attachment between the user and product or provider. The main aim of customer experience management (CEM) is to turn satisfied customers into loyal customers and loyal customers, in turn, into "passionate advocates" for a brand or product.[33] So CEM strives not only for direct effects such as buying intentions, revenue and intensity of use, but very deliberately, too, on indirect effects such as word of mouth and referrals. At best, this should be achieved at every single customer touchpoint.

---

[33] See Schmitt, Bernd: "Customer Experience Management: A Revolutionary Approach To Connecting With Your Customers", 2003, P. 25ff.

Apart from the term 'guest experience', there is also 'guest engagement'. Guest engagement may be regarded as the outcome of a series of guest interactions with a hotel or hotel service that trigger an internal response in the customer. Guest engagement is essentially of a more personal nature and implies the guest's involvement at various levels (rational, emotional, sensual, physical and cognitive).[34]

The benefits of effective guest experience management are obvious. As well as the fact that positive guest experiences constitute a highly effective differentiation feature, properly aligning guest experience management in an organization contributes substantially to increasing revenue. Over their guest life cycle, loyal guests book a preferred brand far more frequently. They are also more open to cross- and up-selling offerings, they actively recommend the brand to others, and they exhibit, at the same time, greater price tolerance. It is also impressive that, according to a study conducted by Oracle, 86 percent of guests are prepared to pay more for a good guest experience.[35] Similarly, 89 percent of guests reject a hotel or hotel brand if they have had a poor experience.

Another benefit of guest experience management is the focus on the guest experiences that are important and really relevant. For example, while guest experience management does indeed,

---

[34] See Herbstritt, Kathrin: "Customer Experience Management: Konzept eines entscheidungsorientierten Managementansatzes im B2B-Dienstleistungsbereich", 2015, P. 6
[35] See Hirt, Michaela / Monard, Frédéric: "Customer Experience Management (CEM) – Kundenerlebnisse aktiv gestalten und steuern", 2013, P. 4

essentially, pursue the goal of delivering positive guest experiences throughout the value creation chain, cost-effectiveness is always taken into consideration, too. Translated to the digital guest experience in the hotel, this means that digital guest experience management leads to a win-win situation for the guest and the hotel – guests' personal experiences generate financial benefit, and guests' digital needs are met. An emotional and, therefore, long-term connection is established between the guests and the hotel.

Only hotels that manage to continuously meet their guests' digital needs during their stay will, over the longer term, be able to differentiate themselves in the marketplace and, through these loyal guests, benefit from increased revenues and new guests generated by referrals. For digital guest experience management to be effective, hotels have to listen to their guests and understand their needs and expectations.

The next chapter will present the various digital guest experience management tools which hotels need to invest in, in the future, in order to satisfy guests' current and future needs.

31

Chapter 3

Digital guest experience tools

3 Digital guest experience tools

Digital guest experience tools are an effective way of interlinking digital and physical channels. This enables guests to be addressed in an effective, efficient way, and leads to optimization in the area of processes, costs and revenues.

The following sections describe, in detail, the various potential digital guest experience tools that may be relevant in a hotel guest's future digital customer journey. They help the hotel to increase revenues, reduce costs and improve guest satisfaction and loyalty.

Here it should be explicitly pointed out that, where we have been unable to provide evidence from research and studies, and where there was no practical evidence, some assumptions have been made in terms of the outcomes of the optimizations we refer to.

We have also attempted to maintain a certain logical order in terms of presentation. Thus the chapter about digital guest experience tools begins with the room assignment challenge at check-in, proceeds to the use of service robots at check-in and the option of taking luggage to the room, and so on. However, because the various digital guest engagement tools are sometimes interlinked and come into recurring contact with the guest during their hotel stay, the chronological sequence of the sub-sections has not always been observed.

3.1 Check-in & digital room assignment

Checking in and assigning the right room are still a process bottleneck. In the hotel industry many things have changed over recent decades, but the way in which rooms are assigned remains, at times, as old as the hotel industry itself.

3.1.1 Definition of digital room assignment

Though hotels switched to electronic reservation systems over 20 years ago, in many hotels rooms continue to be assigned as they always have been.[36] Room assignment tradition goes back to pre-computer days when hotels used a big book or wall rack, sometimes also known as a Whitney Rack.[37] Hotels could check availability by looking at the rack, simply by seeing whether a particular room was available on a particular day, or how many rooms were still vacant that day. In those days guests were assigned a particular room when making their reservation.[38]

With the introduction of software-based property management systems (PMS) and central reservation systems (CRS), the

---

[36] See Gruen, Keith: "Pre-assigning room numbers can lead to lost business", 2013, https://hetras.wordpress.com/tag/room-assignment/

[37] See Ambwani, Meenakshi Verma: "From 'Whitney Rack' to electronic reservation systems", 2013, http://www.thehindubusinessline.com/economy/hospitality-sector-from-whitney-rack-to-electronic-reservation-systems/article5064873.ece

[38] See Kasavana, Michael / Brooks, Richard: "Managing Front Office Operations", 8th Issue, 2009, P. 123-124

management of rooms and their availability was improved.[39] The complex business of revenue management was also digitalized, and these days the Revenue Manager can use revenue management systems (RMS) to adjust rates to external factors (yields) in order to optimize revenue.[40]

In the hotel sector, revenue and yield management is increasingly being regarded as a success factor that enables the hotel business to remain competitive. Yield management is used to adjust rates and capacities dynamically in order to make best use of, and optimize profits from, a specific overall capacity.[41] The main objective here is to attain maximum revenue while, at the same time, preventing a product from becoming degraded.[42]

So yield management is all about utilizing rooms at the highest possible price, supported by technological automation.[43] However, it does not take into account whether rooms are actually being assigned in the optimal way and it fails to take all the influencing factors (including guest-related factors) into consideration. Yield

[39] See O'Conner, Peter: "Using Computers in Hospitality", 3rd edition, 2004, P. 206
[40] See Schulz, Axel: "eTourismus: Prozesse und Systeme: Informationsmanagement im Tourismus", 2nd edition, 2015 , P. 494
[41] See Günther, Pamela: "Yield Management als Erfolgsfaktor der Hotellerie: Eine kritische Evaluation der automatisierten Yield-Management-Systeme", 2013, P. 4
[42] See Bagemihl, Jens: "Die strategische Bedeutung von Yield Management im Hotelgewerbe", 1994, P. 8
[43] See Sölter, Marc: "Hotelvertrieb, Yield-Management und Dynamic Pricing in der Hotellerie", 2007, P. 4

management would also benefit from the deployment of an IT-based, automated room assignment system.

As fully-automated, digital room assignment systems scarcely exist at the moment, the literature says little about them. Neither is there yet an accepted definition. So we shall define digital room assignment as follows:

> *Digital room assignment is the automated, algorithm-based assigning of hotel rooms paying optimal consideration to various influencing factors.*

The various factors (parameters) that the algorithms need to take into account, and their influence on room assignment, will be covered in the next section.

3.1.2 Deploying digital room assignment

The use of digital room assignment is highly complex because different parameters, each with a different weighting and a variety of effects, need to be taken into consideration. We shall now list the different types of parameter and describe their effect in detail:

- **Length of stay**

    The length of stay plays a key role in room assignment. When optimizing room assignment when a reserved room category is booked up, long stays should not be moved into a next-highest category. This allocation would be blocked out for rooms that bring in more revenue which would no longer be available for sale.

- **Future arrivals**

  The more arrivals are expected on any day, the more complex becomes room assignment, and the need for automatic optimization increases. To this extent, the number of future arrivals is a key influencing factor when optimizing room assignment.

- **Bed types**

  If, when making the reservation, a guest asks for a particular type of bed, e.g. queen size, king size or two single beds, or if they have booked a cot for a child, the room assignment needs to take this into account to avoid the guest potentially being dissatisfied.

- **Room features**

  Any room features that are specified or booked when the reservation was made need to be considered when assigning the hotel room. If a guest read about a bath-tub in the room description, or if one were visible in the room photos, and if the guest opted for the room precisely because of this feature, there is bound to be a complaint if the feature is not provided.

- **Price**

When assigning rooms it can be a good idea to put guests who have paid a higher price for their stay in a room in a higher category. One might also imagine excluding employees with personnel discounts from upgrading.

- **Costs**

Because the cost of cleaning a suite is more than for cleaning a standard room, a good room assignment system should only assign suites for upgrades in exceptional circumstances.

- **Number of guests**

The number of guests is a relevant parameter when assigning rooms. A single room cannot be assigned if a couple is coming, and the assignment can only be a room with an extra bed if a small family (one child) is expected. If the room assignment is poor, families in particular can suffer. It is regularly the case that a family room is occupied or does not exist and that family members need to be lodged in two separate rooms. If these rooms are adjacent to one another and mutually accessible via a connecting door, that would of course be acceptable. However, on review portals such as TripAdvisor and HolidayCheck there are many complaints from families who have been given two rooms on two different floors so that they are absurdly far apart.

Groups also appreciate the various rooms being on the same floor. So taking this parameter into account when assigning rooms can also improve guest satisfaction.

- **Booking channel**

To gain an advantage over the OTAs, some hotels note the channel from which the booking has come. If certain rooms are booked out, and if room assignment is optimized, guests who booked their room via the hotel's own website are given the pleasure of a higher room category than those who have come via an OTA. But there are also hotels who pursue a diametrically opposing strategy – it is the OTA bookers who are given an upgrade in the hope that the guest books the hotel again for their stay next time. In this way the hotel aims to set itself apart from competitors on the booking platforms.

- **Company profile**

Many firms have agreed special company rates with hotels and it makes sense that the hotels do not link highly priced room categories to those rates, which are usually lower, or assign them to company personnel. To this extent, this parameter should be taken into consideration when assigning rooms.

▪ **Loyalty level**

When assigning rooms, regular guests need to be treated with particular care. A loyal guest who comes to the hotel once a week and knows the hotel almost always expects their favorite room.[44] A digital room assignment system can be supported in this respect by guest scores that are or should be entered in the CRM system.[45]

If the hotel has a loyalty program, and the guest is a member, the guest can be given their favorite room based on their loyalty level, or they should be given preferential treatment when they need to be upgraded (if lower room categories are booked up).

▪ **Accessibility**

A certain number of rooms in the hotels these days are designed to be accessible. I.e. they are fitted out for users with motor, sensory or cognitive disabilities. This relates, for example, to the size of movement areas and shower areas, and the positioning of features and controls. When

---

[44] See Melzer, Michael: "Tipps und Tricks für den Rezeptionisten: Organisiertes Arbeiten am Hotelempfang", 2014, P. 32

[45] See Gardini, Marco: "Marketing-Management in der Hotellerie", 3rd edition, 2015, P. 325

assigning rooms, these rooms should not be occupied by other people, but rather by those people for whom they are intended. Likewise, it is counter-productive for people with disabilities to be upgraded to a room without disabled facilities.

- **Guest types**

When assigning rooms, care can be taken that business guests or couples are not placed adjacent to, or on the same floor as, families in order to avoid potential complaints about noise.[46] Similarly with guests who only arrive late at night. They should also be grouped together when assigning rooms so that other guests do not have their night-time peace and quiet disturbed. People traveling alone (women and older guests, in particular) could be lodged on lower floors to improve their sense of security, so that they can get to reception more quickly.[47] The same can be said of people who suffer from claustrophobia. These groups can also be placed on the lower floors to reduce the number of steps to their floor.

If a non-smoker is given a smoking room the guest is bound to be dissatisfied, and they will not just form a negative

[46] See Jones, Michael Forrest: "How do hotels assign rooms to guests?", 2012, https://www.quora.com/How-do-hotels-assign-rooms-to-guests
[47] See Weller, Manuel: "Worauf Sie im Hotel achten sollten", 2015, http://biztravel.fvw.de/reisesicherheit-worauf-sie-im-hotel-achten-sollten/1/142953/4081

opinion but could even cancel the room altogether and opt to spend the night with a competitor.

- **Cleanliness and cleaning**

  For hotels with high occupancy rates, this parameter may be disregarded. For all other hotels, however, all the rooms should be assigned at regular intervals. It does not make much sense to withdraw certain rooms from the assignment process and leave them unused or unoccupied for a period. Ultimately, it may be, at a moment of high occupancy, that a guest finds themselves in a room with a layer of dust, or a room that has been unused for a long time might need additional cleaning, which incurs expenditure.

Taking these parameters into consideration, there is a real dilemma when assigning hotel rooms: reception staff and booking agents can only make assumptions that will enable them to make the correct assignment. Because of the complexity of taking all the parameters into account, however, rooms will get booked up and certain room categories will be fragmented. In the end, the guests' requirements will not be met which, in turn, can lead to guest dissatisfaction.

Only digital room assignment systems, based on mathematical algorithms, can completely record all the reservation and guest requirements and ensure optimal room assignment under the given circumstances.

3.1.3 Challenges for digital room assignment

With digital room assignment, the challenge is that, despite all the optimization algorithms, the hotel has to do a certain amount of preliminary work to be successful.

To be able to resolve the dilemma of assigning beds, any irrelevant and duplicated room feature codes need to first be discarded. Of all the available codes, guests usually require fewer than ten. In general, these include the bed type, floor, view and so on.

Once the codes have been reorganized, a clear hierarchy needs to be defined. The importance of the different features in relation to one another needs to be established. I.e., for example, the bed type is given a greater weighting than the floor. This weighting plays a key role in optimizing room assignment with regard to guest satisfaction and increasing revenue. No general formula can be applied, since every hotel will prioritize its own criteria differently.

Not only do features need to be eliminated and prioritized in the PMS and the room assignment system, the room descriptions in the sales channels need to be revised and standardized to avoid leaving guests frustrated by their room assignment. The challenge here is that rooms need to be described with precision so that the necessary features are made clear. The current problem when booking a room online is that a guest books a room on a top floor, with a bath-tub and far from any elevator or from an ice machine. But when the booking is being made it is impossible to know how many such combinations there actually are. There are hardly any providers offering links and interfaces to the various PMS, CRS and room assignment systems.

The fact that the various systems are not mutually integrated can also be a reason preventing the introduction of appropriate systems. A receptionist at check-in will not work with different systems in order to not unnecessarily prolong the check-in. This would be diametrically opposed to the proposed goal of process optimization in terms of check-in waiting time.

Another challenge is the trend, and the guest's desire, to find their hotel room themselves. As is the case with airline companies, guests want to check themselves in online approx. 24 or 36 hours before their arrival and, as they do when selecting seats in a plane, choose their own hotel room. This option can have a major impact on automated room assignment, because certain rooms are blocked out and no longer available for optimization. This is another variable that optimization needs to take into consideration. On the positive side, this can enable an additional charge to be levied on the guest so that more revenue is generated, plus, rooms that have been checked into can be billed in full even though the guest does not then appear.[48] In addition, this service could only be offered to guests participating in the hotel's loyalty program, so that the hotel gets guest data in return. This could create another tool for direct bookings and reduce the number of bookings coming via OTAs. It can also increase guest satisfaction, since the guest has selected

---

[48] See O'Neill, Sean: "Choose your own room, for a fee", 2011, http://www.budgettravel.com/blog/hotels-choose-your-own-room-for-a-fee,11698/

their room themselves without being subject to any uncertainty at check-in.

A challenge that should not be overlooked is the receptionist him/herself. Up to now, it has been the receptionist who has decided which guest is given which room. If digital room assignment is introduced, the system takes over this task and the receptionist feels that their ability to judge the optimal room assignment is being doubted. The front-desk agent may also lose a source of minor income from tips given in gratitude for being upgraded. Moreover, any decision that goes against the system's recommendation can be identified and reported to hotel management. So one may anticipate a certain amount of resistance to the implementation of a digital room assignment system.

3.1.4 Return on investment from digital room assignment

A look at review portals such as TripAdvisor and HolidayCheck reveals that slow check-ins and the disregarding of loyalty statuses lead to complaints. But guests' complaints most frequently relate to the room. According to a study by TrustYou, 52 percent of complaints are about the room.[49]

In this context, digital room assignment comes into its own and provides assistance. With digital room assignment, the return on

---

[49] See anon.: "Was hat Meckerpotenial? Die Top10 der häufigsten
       Beschwerden in Hotels", 2010,
       http://www.trustyou.com/reisebranche/was-hat-meckerpotential-die-
       top10-der-haufigsten-beschwerden-in-hotels?lang=de

investment comes particularly from the areas of cost reduction, revenue increase, process optimization and, above all, greater guest satisfaction.

- **Process optimization**

  Why do check-ins still take so long these days? As stated in the introduction to this book, over half of all hotel bookings now come via the online channel. That means that most of the information about the guest that is required for check-in is already available. One reason for lengthy check-in is that the available rooms are only assigned when guests are checking in, and to do this the receptionist has to navigate around the PMS to find the right room.

  By assigning rooms automatically using pre-defined parameters such as room category, guest preferences, loyalty status, upgrade option and booking channel, the process is hugely optimized for the receptionist. It can also vastly improve the check-in process since there is no more searching the system for a suitable room. The receptionist can check in more guests in the same time, or use the time gained to deal more closely with the newly arrived guest, and provide information about the hotel's restaurant or spa area.

- **Reducing costs and increasing revenue**

As well as saving time at check-in, as we have seen, and the resulting opportunity to spend more time on cross-selling for the restaurant or spa area, a defragmented room inventory also makes it easier for the receptionist to sell an upgrade.

In contrast, optimized room assignment avoids unnecessary upgrades and lost revenue. Downgrades and guest refunds are also reduced. Algorithm-based systems enable cancellations and new bookings to be fed into the room occupancy system in real time and taking the general circumstances into account so that a defragmented room inventory is reduced and occupancy is always revenue-optimized.

- **Guest satisfaction**

Besides reducing costs and increasing revenue, the biggest return on investment comes in the area of guest satisfaction. As mentioned, many complaints and negative ratings on review portals such as TripAdvisor and HolidayCheck relate to check-in, the room and the loyalty status. Optimized room assignment cuts down the waiting time at reception. It also takes into account guests' personal requirements and wishes when assigning rooms. The guest has usually booked a particular room with particular features (double-room with sea view and bath-tub) and is given "their" reserved room. In this way, the guest's expectation is satisfied, which is particularly pleasing for families. A family with two children wants a family room, and not two rooms on two different floors.

Many hotel loyalty schemes include free upgrades based on availability and loyalty status.

If the guest consults the hotel website in their room and sees that a better room category is still available, it can result in irritation, complaints and negative ratings. With automated room assignment, the loyalty status can be taken into account.

Every room assignment optimization has a positive impact on guest satisfaction, on guest loyalty, on ratings and, thus, on revenue too in the medium term. [50] By avoiding unnecessary up- and downgrades, direct cost savings can be made.

---

[50] See anon.: "Die strategische Bedeutung von RevPar und Bewertungen", 2015, http://www.customer-alliance.com/de/strategie-revpar-bewertungen/

3.2 Service robots

3.2.1 Definition of service robots

The increasing capabilities of robot hardware and software, and advances in sensor and actuator technology, are leading to robots being increasingly deployed away from industrial mass production. As is already the case in many production operations, in the service sector too, there is an increasing use of robots that perform tasks partly or fully automatically, thus ensuring that the cost of the task is kept low and the quality high. These service robots differ greatly from one another and are specifically designed for the task concerned.

The use of service robots is mainly an option for simple, monotonous activities that do not require well-trained employees.[51] And also for activities that are repeated frequently but need to remain as high-quality as possible. In such cases using people may often be too expensive or there are not enough people in the labor market.[52]

For our purposes, service robots may be defined as follows:

---

[51] See Ling, Isabel: "Cornell Robotics Startup Revolutionizes Hospitality" in: The Cornell Daily, 2016, http://cornellsun.com/2016/01/29/c-u-robotics-startup-revolutionizes-hospitality/

[52] See Schraft, Rolf Dieter: "Serviceroboter – Innovative Technik in Dienstleistung und Versorgung", 1996, P. 1

> *A service robot is a freely-programmable, moving device that performs services partly or fully automatically.*

Services, here, refers to activities that are not used directly to produce industrial goods, but to deliver services to people and facilities.

While the number of service robots is low compared to the number of industrial robots, they have a great deal of potential. [53] The sections that follow describe potential future deployment areas for service robots in hotels.

3.2.2 Service robots in hotels

Increasing cost pressure in the low priced segment of the hotel industry is forcing many hotels to reduce costs. Robots can clean the hotel corridors, for example, or help with service, so that fewer human employees are required in the future. Savings of between one third and a half of costs can be made in this way, compared with a conventional hotel business.

There are also already ideas for robots at reception, and they will be increasingly used there in the near future. It is highly probable that

---

[53] See The International Federation Of Robotics: "World-Robotics-Studie: Service-Roboter erobern die Welt", 2015, http://www.presseportal.de/pm/115415/3135305

guests will soon be able to check in with intelligent, electronic virtual beings (see Figure 2).

Fig. 2: "Example of a service robot at reception"

Source: Trendsderzukunft.de, 2015

The benefit of reception robots is that guests can easily be received in multiple languages. It can increase guest satisfaction if the guest is greeted, and feels understood, in their own language. With face recognition, robots can identify regular guests and address them in their own language, and also take into account their preferences when choosing a room.

A robot can also perform concierge duties. At check-in the luggage is given the service robot which, without complaining or struggling, takes it to the room. One benefit here is that the guest does not need to worry about how much tip would be appropriate for this service. If the reserved room has not yet been released, the robot will temporarily store the luggage and only take it to the guest's room when housekeeping sends a message (by tablet or smartphone).[54]

Room service, too, would be simplified using robots. Missing towels, lavatory paper, toothpaste, newspapers or even condoms are ordered online and brought to the room by the service robot. Kitchen orders could be delivered straight to the room with no additional personnel. Anyone ordering a meal or something to drink after midnight is only served by the service robot.[55] Mobile food robots could also bring a range of food and drink to the guest's room, or prepare the order right there in the guest's room.

---

[54]   See Gardini, Marco A.: "Marketing-Management in der Hotellerie", 2015, P. 432
[55]   See Graf, René / Weckesser, Peter: "Autonomous roomservice in a hotel" in: "Intelligent Autonomous Vehicle", 1998, P. 501

Fig. 3: "Example of a service robot"
Source: N-TV, 2016

With a rising number of hotel robots and increasing acceptance by hotel guests, the hotel industry could be revolutionized – and humans could be pushed out of a service area where they were previously essential.

But it is not purely in areas of guest contact that service robots will be seen more frequently in the future. Robots will not be kept out of the hotel kitchen, either. British company "Moley Robotics" has already unveiled a fully automated chef that deploys two robot arms fixed above the hot plate, based on human limbs.[56]

Fig. 4: "Robotic kitchen by Moley Robotics"
Source: Digitaltrends.com, 2015

The robotic hands have four fingers and a thumb, and can do everything that a human hand can. The automatic hands are driven by over 20 motors and have a number of sensors to detect position and utilize fingertip touch. Guests can choose from 2,000 recipes

---

[56] For more information, see also: Moley Robotics
http://www.moley.com/

by top cook Tim Anderson.[57] The robot chef is due to go into serial production and be available within a few years.[58]

Though robots will be rarely seen in the kitchens of luxury hotels over the coming years, they offer low-budget hotels a new way of cutting costs while being able to offer high-quality meals.

Robots may be deployed, particularly, on monotonous, time-consuming or heavy tasks such as arranging the seating in a meeting room. Different types of table and chair are taken to a room where they are positioned as required (parliamentary, banquet, blocks, U-shape, etc.), and then removed again after being used.[59]

But even now robot technology can help hotel staff with very specific tasks. For example, a concierge who speaks Chinese can be "teleported" into a so-called "telepresence robot" and assist a guest from China with their problems. The concierge does not need to be physically present in the hotel. In this way, hotel chains can make more effective use of their employees' potential and increase guest satisfaction.

---

[57] See Plass-Fleßenkämper, Benedikt: "In dieser Küche steht ein Roboter hinterm Herd", 2015, https://www.wired.de/collection/tech/moley-robotics-erfindet-den-vollautomatischen-koch

[58] See Pluta, Werner: "Heute kocht der Roboter", 2015, http://www.golem.de/news/moley-robotics-der-roboter-bereitet-das-essen-zu-1504-113511.html

[59] See Schraft, Rolf-Dieter / Volz, Hansjörg: "Serviceroboter: Innovative Technik in Dienstleistung und Versorgung", 1996, P. 98

3.2.3 Future use of service robots in hotels

Without a doubt, the number of hotels around the world that will increasingly turn to service robots of every type is set to increase. The Japanese are at the forefront of this trend. In Sasebo, Japan, in 2016 the robot hotel "Henn-na", which translates as "the unusual hotel" opened. It is located in the Huis Ten Bosch theme park in Sasebo, Nagasaki.[60] But it is particularly hotel chains in the USA that are seeing the enormous potential of service robots and investing in the technology even now. Marriott Hotels are using their "Mario" service robot to welcome guests to the Marriott Hotel in Gent, Belgium.[61] Hilton hotels are using the "Connie" robot as a concierge in Virginia and the InterContinental Group have named their robot "Dash". In low-budget and business hotels with standardized processes, in particular, the next logical step is to use robots.

It could also be, in the future, that human input from real employees in the hotel (for example, at the breakfast buffet, on reception, helping in the spa area or room service) will only be provided if

---

[60] See Hansa, Kira: "Dieses Personal zickt nicht rum und will kein Trinkgeld", 2016,
https://www.welt.de/reise/deutschland/article153085621/Dieses-Personal-zickt-nicht-rum-und-will-kein-Trinkgeld.html

[61] See Douag,Sarah: "Erste humanoide Roboter an der Rezeption" in Hospitality Inside Special Expo Real, 2015, P. 25

actually requested by the guest. This type of "real service" will then be viewed as an add-on and charged as a supplement.[62]

In the future robots will increasingly be able to identify situations autonomously, respond in a suitable way and interact with people in real time. The integration of sensor and actuator technology, communications and computing power is enabling new types of service and application for humans and robots. In the future a robot will be able to detect that a cup is empty and fill it with coffee or – depending on how it is programmed – put it into the dishwasher.

3.2.4 Challenges for the use of service robots

Even though service robots are already capable of doing many things, they also have certain limitations. For instance, every study on the subject, without exception, reports problems and unreliability with voice recognition, particularly in very busy areas, which also causes extremely limited interactivity in some cases.[63] Up to now, this failing has either been compensated for by alternative input types or by restricting the robot system's autonomy by having an operator take over voice recognition on behalf of the

---

[62] See Gardini, Marco A.: "Marketing-Management in der Hotellerie", 2015, P. 432
[63] See Czarnetzki, Stefan: "Allgemeine Akzeptanz von Servicerobotern", 2016, P. 7

only partly-autonomous system. Face recognition software is also sometimes still deficient when lighting conditions are tricky.[64]

But research and development should not only focus on overcoming technological challenges. The challenge of hotel guests' acceptance of service robots, in particular, stands alongside technical challenges. Acceptance in terms of whether and how people allow themselves to be served and helped by robots differs greatly from culture to culture. In social terms Europe and Germany, in particular, is a land of techno-skeptics.[65] Trust is greatest in Japan, where robots have been in use for longer.[66] There is little or no technology skepticism in Japan, and in no other country do people feel so benevolent towards robots.[67]

Ideally, potential users would be involved early when developing service robots. This would make it easier to develop service robots that are accepted more widely and perceived as a help rather than a threat.

---

[64] See Hellrung, Niels et al.: "Einbettung assistierender Technologien in Gesundheitsnetzwerke" in: Leimeister, Jan Marco: "Technologiegestützte Dienstleistungsinnovation in der Gesundheitswirtschaft", 2012, P. 283

[65] See anon.: "Service-Roboter: Kühle Drinks vom elektronischen Barkeeper", 2012, http://www.handelsblatt.com/technik/forschung-innovation/service-roboter-noch-fehlt-die-akzeptanz-fuer-die-service-maschinen/7259486-2.html

[66] See Schmidt, Holger: "Menschen vertrauen Robotern oft blind", 2016, https://netzoekonom.de/2016/11/15/12236/

[67] The positive sentiment towards robots may stem from the Shinto religion which is common in Japan, and in which objects are also regarded and honoured as deities.

Improving the interplay of human and robot in terms of security components is also highly influential in accepting and effectively using service robots.

A financial challenge is also involved in using service robots in hotels. The absence of funding options, in particular, is a barrier. Robot manufacturers need, firstly, to standardize in order to cut costs (procurement and maintenance) and, secondly, consider new business models that also include a funding or leasing model.[68]

3.2.5 Return on investment of service robots

Besides the long-term cost savings for the hotel business, there are undoubtedly, initially, competitive advantages to be gained. There is also the chance to improve guest satisfaction in some areas, and to use the usage data acquired to, in turn, optimize services.

▪ **Cost reduction**

The cost savings in the personnel area are obvious and are probably the main reason for deploying service robots. One practical application that already exists can illustrate this: perfectly folded cloth napkins are essential to any invitingly laid table. In an average hotel business, an average of 400,000 napkins are required every year. If it takes about 30 seconds to fold each one, this important yet monotonous

---

[68] See Klingler-Deiseroth, Carmen: "Serviceroboter gewinnen an Marktreife", 2014, http://www.vdi-nachrichten.com/Technik-Wirtschaft/Serviceroboter-gewinnen-an-Marktreife

activity consumes up to 3,333 working hours per year. Robots could be used to do this in the future.

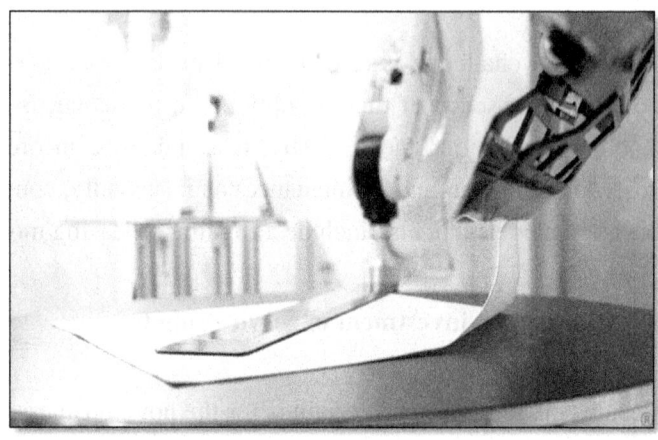

Fig. 5: "Example of napkin-folding robot"
Source: DENSO Europe B.V., 2015

As described in previous sections, robots can clean hotel corridors, remove trash from rooms, take items of clothing in the cloakroom or help out with service, thus cutting spending on staff. This could save between one-third and half of costs compared with a conventional hotel operation. Robots also offer greater productivity, since they are available around the clock. Periods of illness and vacation are partly cancelled out by breakdown and maintenance periods.[69]

One may assume from this that 35 percent of jobs could be replaced by intelligent robots over the next 20 years.[70]

- **Competitive advantage**

As service robots begin to be rolled out, in particular, using them can still be a unique selling feature for the hotel and thereby provide a competitive advantage. Tech-savvy guests may even opt for a hotel with a service robot to test them out. Room service revenues can increase when service robots begin to be deployed as many guests will order food and drink to their room precisely because of the robots, to try them out.[71]

Another competitive advantage comes from staff being able to spend more time on the guests as the service robots cut down on monotonous, time-consuming jobs. This extra time for the guest can generate a distinct advantage vis-à-vis competitors.

---

[69] See anon.: "Wettbewerbsvorteile durch Robotics realisieren" in: "Detecon Management Report", Issue 2, 2016, P. 32f.
[70] See Frey, Carl Benedikt / Osborne, Michael A.: "The Future of Employment", 2013, P. 38ff.
[71] See Hansa, Kira: Loc. cit.

New sources of revenue can be generated in the events and conferences area. A hotel can provide telepresence robots and the event organizers can hire them to enable conference delegates to participate remotely. This could also provide new sources of income for event organizers.

- **Guest satisfaction**

Service robots are capable of understanding different languages and articulating different languages. If a guest is greeted at reception, and feels understood, in their own language, guest satisfaction can increase. If the guest is recognized using face recognition and database matching, any preferences in terms of room assignment or meal recommendations can be taken into account.[72] This high level of service quality will be reflected in the guest's satisfaction over the short or medium term.

The robots can also collect data relating to guest satisfaction: when a service, such as a club sandwich or a missing towel, has been delivered, the robot can ask on a display whether the guest was satisfied or whether there is room for improvement.

With intelligent voice recognition, so-called keyword alerts can be set up. When service robots detect these keywords

---

[72] See Stampfl, Nora: "Die Zukunft der Dienstleistungsökonomie: Momentaufnahme und Perspektiven", 2011, P. 144

in their vicinity (for example, expressions with negative connotations), they can address a dissatisfied guest and try to help them.[73]

It is crucial that all the data generated on guests' satisfaction and dissatisfaction is analyzed and drawn upon to optimize the service.

---

[73] See Friedlander, R.J.: "Are Robots Changing the Way That Guest Experience is Measured in the Hotel Industry?", 2016, http://www.4hoteliers.com/features/article/99984hoteliers.com

3.3 Digital signage

3.3.1 Definition of digital signage

The term "digital signage" is confusing and has not been clearly defined. Different terms have become established for the same concept, varying according to region and sector. Besides digital signage, at the point of sale the terms digital media, instore TV and narrowcasting have also been used.[74] The term digital signage is often used where flat screens or other display devices are used to present moving images. But this reduction to a pure presentation system with no networking or Internet connection would not do justice to the possibilities that digital signage now offers.[75]

While the issue of digital signage is an ongoing issue in the digital marketing (out-of-home media) area, it is not new. Depending on one's perspective, digital signage has existed since 1984. That was when the Canadian food chain Loblaws first used Sony televisions in their shops to show the latest adverts.[76] And who is not familiar with product ads in DIY stores, which have been commonplace for years?

---

[74] See Telschow, Stephan: "Digital Signage – die Kommunikationsrevolution am Point Of Sale" in: Gesellschaft für Innovative Marktforschung Update 1, 2010, P. 2

[75] See Fischer, Peter: "Digital Signage – Werbliche Kommunikation am Point of Sale auf Flachbildschirmen. Theoretische Hintergründe, Aufgaben und Wirkungsmessungen.", 2010, P. 18

[76] See Schnitzlein, Maximilian: "Grundlagen des Digital Signage", 2015, P. 3

To understand the opportunities that digital signage offers the hotel industry, the first step is to define more precisely what digital signage actually is. For this purpose there is a statement which is valid in general terms, that digital signage combines the three media TV, online and outdoor advertising. It is an out-of-home medium with the look and feel of television and wide coverage which offers control options as in the online sector.[77]

The above definition is a good description of digital signage, but to understand it one requires some basic knowledge of the digital advertising sector.

As a basis for what follows, therefore, we shall define digital signage in a simplified way, as follows:

> *Digital signage is a digitally networked, visually appealing display system for presenting information.*

Whether this information is of a commercial or non-commercial character is irrelevant to the definition. For use in hotels, the commercial character – i.e. the relevance of potential revenue increases – should definitely play the more significant role.

---

[77] See Tezlaff, Jutta: "Digital Signage schafft neue Möglichkeiten für die Markenkommunikation am Point of Sale" in: "Marke 41" No. 5, 2008, P. 81

3.3.2 Digital signage in hotels

Digital signage systems are already being used in hotels. The TVs in hotel rooms, in particular, are used for digital signage. The default television channel that appears when the guest switches on tells the guest about particular hotel facilities, offerings in the hotel restaurant and its opening times, or shows trailers for the Pay TV program. All the information is aimed at generating additional revenue.

But digital signage long ago passed from hotel rooms to other areas of the hotel. In the conference and events sector, digital signage systems are used as signposts for conference delegates. Monitors placed at reception, outside conference rooms and at other strategic locations tell delegates which event location they are visiting and how to get there. But the large displays also show business travelers flight and rail information.[78]

---

[78] See anon.: "Interactive Digital Signage helps guests find their way" in: "Lodging" No. 34, 2008, P. 60

Fig. 6: "Example of digital signage in a hotel"
Source: isignage.io, 2016

Studies show that digital signage systems have the ability to not only show images with vivid colors, but also to attract the viewer (here the hotel guest) like a magnet via films with sound. The key here, though, is that the systems offer information that is useful, concise and relevant.[79]

This means that the digital spaces are ideally used for internal advertising campaigns. So a hotel should show different offerings at different times. This could include spa treatments, special offers in the hotel restaurant, golf or tennis courses or events in the hotel

---

[79] See Yackey, Bill: "Digital Signage in the Hotel Industry", 2012, P. 5

that the guest can be offered – similar to the offerings on the television in the hotel room.

The advertising space can also be given to external partners.[80] There already exist many showcases or poster options for local partners such as jewelers, limo services and small theaters. These spaces can be digitalized so that it is always the partner's latest offer or goods that are shown.[81] Using modern advertising technologies, ads will, in the future, be shown on the digital signage systems' ad spaces according to the time of day and day of the week, plus the advertiser's willingness to pay.[82]

In the sense of the digital guest experience, digital signage can also be used to share the guest's individual experience with other hotel guests. For example, content generated by other guests can be shown on the digital signage devices. This would mean that digital signage is acting as a social hub and showing guests' social media posts. A photo flagged on Instagram, a post about the hotel on Facebook, or a tweet on Twitter is thus made available to other hotel

---

[80] See Schaeffler, Jimmy: "Digital Signage: Software, Networks, Advertising, and Displays. A Primer for Understanding the Business", 2013, P. 213

[81] See O'Meara, Lenore: "Hotels struggle to manage electronic communications" in: Hospitality Technology No. 14, 2010, P. II

[82] See Telschow, Stephan: "Im Dialog mit dem Shopper" in: Markenartikel No. 6, 2010, P. 101

guests so that their decision to opt for the hotel is reinforced. This can prevent rejection.[83]

3.3.3 Digital signage outside the hotel

The number of digital signage systems at infrastructure nodes such as airports and railway stations is increasing all the time. These systems are not only being used purely as information boards on which nearby hotels purchase and show their own advertisements.

According to forecasts, the demands on screen content will continue to rise, meaning that digital signage requirements will grow.[84] Over the short or long term it will no longer be enough to simply project content on screens. With interactive digital signage systems, passers-by will become part of digital signage – they will be interacting instead of reacting. This will provide the opportunity for customers in shops, or after the shop has closed, to find their own information, shop online and take part in competitions and discount campaigns.

Many digital signage systems already take the form of interactive kiosk systems. So it seems likely that hotel room rates will also be displayed on the systems in the city and that potential guests are notified about potential offerings or standard prices. The prices can

---

[83] See Kroeber-Riel, Werner / Gröppel-Klein, Andrea: "Konsumentenverhalten", 10th, revised, updated and expanded edition, 2013, P. 96 and 296ff.

[84] See Gründel, Verena: "Digital-Signage-Trends 2015: So erobern Interaktive den Crosschannel-Markt." in: iBusiness, 2014, P. 23

even be changed after each incoming flight or train, thereby opening up an entirely new method of rate yielding based on the target group arriving. Direct bookings could also be made in the digital signage kiosk itself, with the guest being sent their reservation confirmation either by email, SMS or Bluetooth straight to the relevant app on their smartphone.

3.3.4 Challenges for digital signage

The technical implementation in the hotel is undoubtedly a major challenge. The biggest challenge for digital signage systems comes not from technology but from the content that is to be shown. 'Content is king' is also true of digital signage![85]

A content strategy usually needs to be drawn up from scratch as digital signage brings with it new contents requirements. Existing content may constitute a good starting point, but it cannot be adopted regardless. [86] The expectations that the viewers (hotel guests) have of the information display are high. Given that televisions get better all the time, they are used to getting good, high-quality images. So a PowerPoint presentation created by an intern should not be played on digital signage screens haphazardly and without due consideration. If used like this, digital signage would not produce the success required.[87] Digital signage ought to

---

[85] See Kelsen, Keith: "Unleashing The Power Of Digital Signage", 2010, P. 48
[86] See Kaup, Michael: "Chancen und Risiken von Digital Signage", 2010, P. 77
[87] See Kelsen, Keith: ibid, 2010, P. 86

be regarded as a marketing tool in just the same way as newspapers and TV are. Advertisements in those media are also produced professionally, as ad placement costs are high and they need to be delivered effectively to the viewer.

However, there is one difference compared with showing TV adverts – digital signage content ought to also work, and be understood by the viewer, with no sound.

Besides displaying information in a professional way, the technical circumstances also need to be taken into account when generating content. If more than one screen is to be used, with different sizes and formats – for example, a 42-inch screen in landscape format and a 32-inch screen in portrait format – it will make showing content more complex and be a greater challenge for the hotel.[88] One of the hotel's requirements should be that no additional content management system (CMS) has to be used and maintained. In the future there has to be a CMS that is independent both of the platform and the output medium. This development is not yet at an end, but it will mean that in a few years' time so-called cross-media publishing systems will be used to centrally manage all the data.[89]

The content also needs to be distributed to the devices. With modern digital signage systems this is done using WLAN (Wi-Fi) or LAN and content is fed in centrally. However, there either has to be a

---

[88] On this, see also Schaeffler, Jimmy: "Digital Signage – Software, Networks, Advertising, and Displays: A Primer for Understanding the Business", 2013, P. 17ff.
[89] See Rotberg, Florian: "Digital Signage-Markt 2010", 2010, P. 13

LAN connection wherever the digital signage system is set up or a functioning, stable WLAN (Wi-Fi).

To this extent, it is clear to see that using digital signage is not only an issue for the hotel's marketing department. The IT department is also involved in planning and operating digital signage solutions. The hotel might also need to call on an interior architect or interior designer.

With larger installations of digital signage solutions, therefore, a pilot should first be organized to see how the different departments work together and, if it is successful, the project can be rolled out systematically.[90]

To round off this section, it should be pointed out that using digital signage constitutes an investment in terms of time and money. Savings should not be made in the wrong place, and professional systems, providers and advisers should be used. A small flat screen at reception, with a PowerPoint display, may be a start, but it is not a good, profitable digital signage solution.

3.3.5 The future of digital signage

With technologies such as gesture control, touchscreen use, Bluetooth beacons, radio frequency identification (RFID) and QR code integration, digital signage is set to become far more

---

[90]   See Hütz, Stefanie: "Erst der Content, sonst kein Vergnügen" in: Stores+Shops Extra Digital Signage Trends No. 6, 2014, P. 44

widespread in the future. Interaction between the transmitter and one or more receivers may even be possible. The hotel will get direct feedback on its campaign and will be able to adjust it or realign it immediately. The guest will feel involved and probably pay even more attention to the medium as a result of the interaction. [91]

But it is face recognition that will become particularly important. Prototypes of digital signage systems with cameras are already being tested on pilot projects. With face recognition, adverts on digital signage systems can be matched precisely to the current viewer. The principle is simple: the integrated camera is used to detect the person's gender and approximate age, and the ad for that specific target group is triggered. The same applies to recognizing groups and identifying ethnicity.[92]

Using face recognition together with available personal data enables advertising messages to be delivered even more effectively.[93] It is plausible that, in the future, the guest's face will be compared in real time with social media data from Facebook, Twitter or Instagram, the guest will be identified and that profile data stored in the CRM system will be added. Using this data bespoke, targeted communication can be delivered and the digital

---

[91] See Samsung whitepaper: "Zeichen der Zeit – Digital Signage als Werbe- und Informationsmedium der Zukunft", 2013, P. 12

[92] See anon.: Signbox Microsystems: "Digital Signage Facial Recognition with signEye", 2016, https://signbox.tv/digital-signage-products/digital-signage-facial-recognition

[93] See Geiger, Harley Lorenz: "A Standard for Digital Signage Privacy" in: Müller, Jörg et al.: "Pervasive Advertising", 2011, P. 106

signage system can suggest highly personalized offerings to the guest.

The lobby lighting may also feasibly be adjusted based on the weather. The digital signage solution would respond flexibly to the guests' moods and run a so-called mood management system.[94] Bright color tones display when it is rainy and stormy, and a cooling atmosphere when the temperatures outside are high. This would, of course, be completely automated, without a hotel employee needing to intervene.

3.3.6 Return on investment of digital signage

As with any stationary system, it is difficult to directly assign a return on investment from using digital signage solutions.[95] However, there is already research which offers evidence that the product acquired leads directly to increased revenue.[96] Germany's GfK (Association for Consumer Research) reported a gain of 16 to 24 percent from deploying digital signage in supermarkets, and a Nielsen consumer survey showed a 33 percent increase in revenue from branded items advertised. In some cases sales of advertised products rose by many times this.

---

[94] See Haderlein, Andreas: "Die digitale Zukunft des stationären Handels: Auf allen Kanälen zum Kunden", 2nd edition, 2013, P. 74
[95] See anon.: "Password to Marketers Meeting: Digital" in: "The World Street Journal", 2007, P. 4
[96] See Fischer, Peter: "Digital Signage – Werbliche Kommunikation am Point of Sale auf Flachbildschirmen. Theoretische Hintergründe, Aufgaben und Wirkungsmessungen", 2010, P. 159 -160

Awareness of the products advertised is also very high with digital signage.[97]

A direct, invisible revenue factor is undoubtedly the sale of costly advertising space to third parties, i.e. either to local companies such as the jeweler or the neighborhood theater, and to large companies like auto manufacturers, car hire companies, taxi firms and airlines.

As well as looking at additional income, the effect of cost savings should not be overlooked. Information boards that need to be written by hand and are disposed of after a single use are no longer needed. Fewer employees are also required to keep repositioning this information board or to provide information, as the digital signage systems will take on this task.

Guest satisfaction, too, is an element that is tough to calculate. In the past there were, without a doubt, a certain number of stressed guests who had to wait in long lines at reception just to ask where their seminar room was.[98] With digital signage solutions this guest group should be more satisfied and may recommend the hotel as being particularly guest-friendly.

---

[97] See Samsung whitepaper: "Zeichen der Zeit – Digital Signage als Werbe- und Informationsmedium der Zukunft", 2013, P. 5

[98] See Eichborn, Marcus: "Kundenzufriedenheit verbessern: Beispiel Digital Signage in Hotels", 2015, http://www.videro.com/magazin/trends-news/kundenzufriedenheit-verbessern-beispiel-digital-signage-hotels

3.4 Concierge tablets

3.4.1 Definition of concierge tablets

There has been increasing use of digital guest folders in hotels over recent years. So-called roompads or suitepads are also known as concierge tablets and do not just replace the traditional guest folder, but offer the hotel a digital touchpoint for marketing activities and promoting sales measures to the guest.

Fig. 7: "Example of a concierge tablet"
Source: Hottelling.net, 2014

As there is a lack of literature about digital guest folders and concierge tablets, no generally applicable definition can be derived and we shall initially define concierge tablets as follows:

Concierge tablets are tablet computer-based interactive solutions that give the hotel guest general information about the hotel and the hotel's services in digital form.

The sections that follow explain which potential information and services are involved.

3.4.2 Using concierge tablets in the hotel

Concierge tablets are particularly useful to the hotel as a marketing tool to sell products and services, and to increase customer loyalty. A concierge tablet should be an integrated tablet solution available to the guest in every hotel room. The in-room tablet PC is integrated into the business's ordering system, can be used to control room features (lighting, drapes, air-conditioning, etc.), and used for entertainment, and it replaces, for example, the guest folder, alarm clock and advertising display. [99]

A range of newspapers and books may also be added to the tablet so that the guest can read the daily paper in their room. In this way, not only does the hotel provide an additional service, it also improves its image in terms of reducing waste paper and environmental friendliness.

---

[99] See Gertschen, Alex: "In-House-Apps für die Hotel Gäste" in: "fokus, htr hotel revue", No.17, 2013, P. 12

With the concierge tablet, guests can be in direct contact with the hotel and, for example, use live chat to raise any issues with the concierge. This enables the concierge to deal with multiple queries at the same time, which makes the concierge's work more effective in large hotels in particular, and can improve guest satisfaction. The latest technology can be used to translate these queries automatically. In the case of complaints, in particular, the ability to respond directly to them is an opportunity that has to be used and usually then also impacts positively on the hotel's rating.

Vice-versa, the hotel can be in direct though discreet contact with the guest and have them take part, for example, in a survey or ask about their preferences, with a view to entering them in the CRM and using them for future stays.

3.4.3 Challenges for concierge tablets

One of the major challenges to the use of concierge tablets is the hotel's own WLAN. Any hotelier who takes the trouble and enters search terms such as "login hotel Wi-Fi" or "Wi-Fi login page" into Google will be astonished by the results. Over 500,000 search results, of which most are forum posts with complaints and problems related to the hotel's WLAN (Wi-Fi).[100] This illustrates the potential and the challenges that exist with Wi-Fi in the hotel industry.[101]

---

[100] Date of access 09.11.2016
[101] See Schulz, Axel / Weithörner, Uwe / Goecke, Robert: "Informationssysteme im Tourismus", 2010, P. 82

A concierge tablet can lead to a fall in complaints relating to problems with the Wi-Fi, as the technology is optimally aligned between the hotel network and the tablet when it is installed, and because the tablet is automatically logged in. So the hotel guest can browse their own devices online and access emails via web clients without any connecting being required.

As with digital signage, so too with the tablets, the underlying content management system (CMS) presents a challenge. As the content display on the tablet is usually determined by the providers, content editing in the underlying CMS is restricted. Often, only photos and text can be shared and changed. In deploying the CMS it should be noted that the hotel staff should be able to make as many changes as possible, to avoid submitting costly change requests to the tablet provider. However, the hotel's staff need to be given adequate training in the use of the CMS. Photos in the wrong format or with a sub-optimal resolution can rapidly have a negative impact on the guest's experience with the tablet, thus endangering the overall success in terms of revenue and guest satisfaction.

The tablet in the hotel room should not merely provide information, but also sell additional hotel services. There is a major challenge here. For a problem-free process and a convincing guest experience, interfaces to the hotel's other systems are required. Orders for room service need to get to the kitchen, table reservations for the restaurant and the controls for the hotel room's features need to work well.[102]

Particular care and attention also need to be given to IT security. If the tablet is connected to the hotel system, a criminal guest may manage to circumvent the tablet's software and get access to the hotel system. They could then reduce their own bill, take control of other hotel rooms' controls, or access other guests' data. In this context, both the tablet providers and the hotel systems providers need to take appropriate security measures.

3.4.4 Return on investment of concierge tablets

The fact is that the concierge tablet is a digital guest touchpoint and should not only replace the traditional guest folder, but generate additional revenue for the hotel. The following are some of the possibilities, but it is not claimed that they the only ones:

- **Room services**

    The ordering of food and drinks to the hotel room is undoubtedly the most obvious way of using the concierge tablet. Guests can send their orders straight to the kitchen from the digital menu. The tablet also enables photos, and even short videos, for showing the meals.

---

[102] Schüffler, Christine: "Supply Management in der Hotelbrache. Grundlagen, Erfolgsfaktoren und Gestaltungsempfehlungen", 2008, P. 239

Other services, such as ironing, laundry and shoe-shine, can also be ordered straight from the tablet.

- **Restaurant visits**

  Hotels can digitalize their entire food menu for the hotel restaurant and show it on a concierge tablet. Care should be taken to make full use of the digital presentation options, as was explained above in the section on room service. Besides using photos of the meals, extra information such as the ingredients of the meal and the drinks can also be displayed. The tablet can also be used to recommend appropriate wines.[103] It should particularly be pointed out that there should not just be a full display of the meals on offer, but also some insight into the inside of the restaurant. Business travelers, in particular, should be encouraged to go to the restaurant rather than use room service.

  It could also be that hotel guests who use the concierge tablet to reserve a table in the restaurant are given a discount voucher or a welcome drink as an aperitif, on the hotel. Ultimately, the tablet should be used to get the guest to visit the hotel's own restaurant rather than drifting off to nearby restaurants.

---

[103] See anon.: "Restaurants der Zukunft: Persönlicher Service weiterhin sehr wichtig" in: "Gastronomie und Hotellerie", 2016, http://www.gastronomie-hotellerie.com/restaurants-der-zukunft-persoenlicher-service-weiterhin-sehr-wichtig

Thus the concierge tablet offers a return on investment in terms of increasing the hotel restaurant's occupancy and increasing guests' spending within the hotel.

- **Spa treatments**

As with the restaurant's offerings, the hotel's spa options are also presented on the concierge tablet and there is an option to book a spa treatment directly.

Hotel guests are often reluctant to visit the hotel spa because, for one thing, they do not know where it is, or they fear that there will be no treatment windows available during their stay, or they think that a treatment is too expensive. The tablet can eliminate these concerns and thereby increase the use of the hotel's spa area.

- **Golf course bookings**

If the hotel has a golf course, the concierge tablet should show it in detail. Besides basic information such as the green fee, discounts and type, some hotels are offering virtual rounds and even virtual flights above the course.

It is undoubtedly unlikely that the tablet in the hotel room will be used to book a golf vacation in the short term. After all, the guest needs to have brought their own golf equipment with them. But the multimedia information will provide inspiration for future stays. And if there is a driving range with hire equipment, the concierge tablet can be used to generate additional revenue.

- **Cinema or theater tickets**

The real concierge, close to reception, is often asked to get theater or cinema tickets. Guests are also interested in restaurant recommendations and shopping options in the neighborhood.[104] The hotel does not normally generate any significant income from these, but commission from recommending restaurants and selling tickets could generate an extra source of revenue. Guest satisfaction should not be disregarded, either, in the context of this service.

Guests themselves can carry out these activities using a concierge tablet. Trailers for the recommended films could be played on the tablet, and the tickets purchased straight from the tablet, as the guest is accustomed to do at home. Guests can also be given restaurant recommendations on the tablet, with the hotel's own restaurant always being highlighted. When a table is reserved at a recommended restaurant outside the hotel, the hotel gets commission from the restaurant based on the reservation itself or the subsequent visit to the restaurant. This does not adversely affect the guest's satisfaction, as they still get the

---

[104] See Andrews, Sudhier: "Hotel Front Office – A Training Manual", 3rd edition, 2013, P. 212f.

information they want. Usually more quickly and in a more personalized form than from the real concierge in the lobby.

- **Sightseeing tours**

  As with tickets for the theater or cinema and restaurant recommendations, acting as an intermediary for sightseeing tours of the city is one of the concierge's duties. If guests themselves are able to research different sightseeing options on the tablet, the concierge's workload is reduced. The tablet also offers the capability to display content in a more emotional way than a concierge can. Recommendations from other hotel guests could also enrich the sightseeing offering.

  If the concierge tablet is used to book a sightseeing tour, the hotel receives a commission from the provider.

- **Merchandising shop**

  A merchandising shop can also be integrated on the concierge tablet. I.e. the guest can order online the hotel's own branded items such as bath-robes and umbrellas. Decorative elements in the hotel room (lamps, cushions, photos or bedding) could also be sold in the online shop. This would be a new source of income for the hotel.

- **Hotel room bookings**

  While in the room, the hotel guest can conveniently use the tablet to plan and book their next stay. It could also be, in the future, that only special rates are shown on the tablet, so that the guest gets a certain price advantage when they make their booking.

As concierge tablets are not yet in widespread use there are, as yet, no reliable findings and no case study with sound results related to increases in revenue or cost savings.

Besides the hotel's own offerings, the sale of advertising space can also be an additional source of income. For example, the spaces can be leased to partners such as car hire companies or airlines, or to the neighborhood theater or cinema. The advertising displays on the concierge tablet can be optimized by clever yield management or personalization options.

With return on investment, the question of the investment required is obvious. It is advantageous that most providers, such as Suitepad, Roompad, Tabero, IQ Pad and iFrontdesk, provide their service on a monthly cost basis. To this extent, there is no great investment in terms of purchasing the devices. Similarly, the hotel suffers no loss if a tablet is damaged or stolen. The provider's insurance covers this. Generally with leasing models, there is always the risk that leasers spend more over the lifetime of the contract than if they had purchased the devices themselves. But it should be noted, in this respect, that tablets are subject to some aging. This means that it is

85

perfectly possible that the provider will replace devices with newer models after three or four years.

As well as the additional sources of income, a concierge tablet also saves resources and costs. Commission costs with OTAs can certainly be saved if a guest uses the concierge tablet to book their next stay while in the hotel itself. The main savings, though, are the costs that have previously been incurred in producing traditional guest folders. We should mention here not only the cost of printing and binding, but in particular the huge saving on paper. Environmental factors and sustainability are also significant here. There is no longer a need to produce flyers for the hotel's restaurant, bar and spa area. Spending on newspapers and magazines can be cut drastically.[105]

Neither is updating content now an onerous task, as information can be changed rapidly in the content management system – as is the case with websites. In this way, the digital guest folder is always completely up to date.

In theory, the concierge tablet can also use an installed IP-based telephone application to replace the fixed line in the hotel room.[106] Neither is an alarm service required any longer, as an integrated alarm assumes this function. If the technology is configured

---

[105] See SuitePad GmbH press release, 2013, http://www.suitepad.de/wp-content/uploads/2013/10/Service-that-sells-Wie-Concierge-Tablets-zu-mehr-Zusatzverk%C3%A4ufen-im-Hotel-f%C3%BChren.pdf

[106] See anon.: "Suitepads dürfen Telefone im Hotelzimmer ersetzen", 2015, http://www.gastronomie-hotellerie.com/suitepads-duerfen-telefone-im-hotelzimmer-ersetzen

appropriately, the tablet can automatically open the curtains and have the guest awoken by sunlight instead of by a shrill alarm. The tablet can also provide visual support for security announcements.

Last but not least the workload on reception staff and the concierge is reduced, as the tablet in the hotel room provides a great deal of information about the hotel and the hotel's neighborhood, or the destination, so that many of the guests' questions are answered without them needing to call reception. So reception staff can busy themselves with other tasks.

This could cut waiting times at check-in and improve guest satisfaction, both at reception and in the room.[107]

To this extent, using concierge tablets can optimize internal processes. Besides the example mentioned, the reduction in workload for reception staff, guests' queries can also be directed to the relevant employee (e.g. in engineering). Resources are no longer required to distribute flyers in the hotel rooms, change newspapers or manually switch the traditional paper guest folders when they are altered. Using the option to pay the hotel bill with the tablet will further shorten the check-out process and it may be optimized to the point where the entire check-out can be done with the tablet.

---

[107] See Hennig, Carsten: "Tablets sind nun Rezeptionist und Concierge im Hotel der Zukunft" in: "Hotelling", 2014, https://hottelling.net/2014/10/20/tablets-sind-nun-rezeptionist-und-concierge-im-hotel-der-zukunft-hetras-und-suitepad-starten-pilotprojekt-im-new-generation-hotel-ruby-sofie-vienna/

Finally, though, it should be pointed out that it is the guests who will determine the success or failure of the concierge tablet. Only if guests use the product will they engage with the hotel's services, book them, and become more loyal customers.

3.4.5 The future

Hong Kong company Think Labs has gone one step further with their "Handy" product. With the "Handy", hotels give their guests the option to take away the digital guest folder during their stay – to have it always with them, as it were.[108]

As well as the existing benefits of digital guest folders in tablet form, being location-independent adds to the functionalities. Now guests can have a navigation device with them without using up their data volume. On international trips, in particular, this offers distinct added value. Sights worth seeing (with a description) can be pre-installed and enable guests to explore the area around the hotel.

Similarly, whenever they wish, guests can contact the hotel free of charge, order a taxi or call a shuttle, if they are unable to find the way back or if it is too far.

And vice-versa, hotels can use push messages to contact their guests or take calls. There is also the option to use the devices', or guests',

---

[108] See Dolcourt, Jessica: "This truly is a handy phone", 2016, https://www.cnet.com/news/handy-phone-gives-travelers-free-data/

movement profiles for data analytics purposes and plan marketing campaigns with partner companies (e.g. restaurants or bars in the vicinity) in a targeted manner.

Fig. 8: "Example of a "Handy" in the hotel room"
Source: etbtravelnews.com, 2016

That digital guest folders will become the norm is apparent due to the benefits described and society's digitalization. But how keen guests will be to take a loaned smartphone from the hotel with them is not clear at the moment and difficult to predict.

3.5 Beacons

3.5.1 Definition of beacons

"Beacon", or "iBeacon", is a term introduced by American company Apple in 2013 to refer to a wireless communication technology based on Bluetooth.[109] As lighthouses do, at regular intervals beacons send information packets in the form of electronic signals to Bluetooth-capable mobile devices, for example Internet-capable smartphones, within a radius of a maximum of 100 meters. The smartphone owner receives a push message with relevant information when they reach a particular location.[110]

So beacons are defined here as follows:

> *Beacons are small electronic transmitters that can send a message via Bluetooth to mobile devices in the vicinity.*

A prerequisite here is that the customer has a corresponding app installed on their mobile phone or tablet and has permitted the settings required. Besides Apple, Google's Android supports the required Bluetooth low energy standard (version 4.3 and higher).

---

[109] See Schmidl, Christian: "Neue Technologien in der mobilen Kundenansprache am Flughafen München" in: Linnhoff-Popien, Claudia / Zaddach, Michael / Grahl, Andreas: "Marktplätze im Umbruch – Digitale Strategien für Services im Mobilen Internet", 2015, P. 229

[110] See Clausen, Elke: "Digitale Transformation - So revolutionieren Sie Ihre Leadgenerierung: Auf Messeerfolg programmiert", 2016, P. 96

Microsoft Windows Phone does not currently allow beacon communication.[111]

Fig. 9: "Example of a beacon"
Source: Beaconwinkel.nl, 2015

The hotelier can easily attach the beacons themselves to just about anywhere they want, e.g. to corridor walls, the hotel bar, hotel room doors or the reception desk, from where they then emit signals. In the most common devices (beacons) power is supplied by batteries that promise to last for two years on average.

---

[111] See Blischke, Johannes: "Betriebssysteme für Smartphones", 2015, P. 48

With the rapid adoption of mobile devices such as smartphones and smartwatches (and other wearables), users' expectations have also changed. They expect, always and everywhere, to be able to access the information or particular services that they want, no matter what the end device, always tailored to the relevant usage context and, at best, without the user having to actively intervene.[112]

Most tech-savvy customers are actively online around the clock and, as such, demanding when it comes to mobile services. This sense of entitlement also exists during their hotel stay, of course.[113] For these requirements, beacons are an excellent technology, and the following sections will describe in detail their benefits and their many areas of application in the hotel industry.

3.5.2 Using beacons in the hotel

Beacons can be used to offer hotel guests special added value and to generate more potential revenue. Beacons can simplify processes in the hotel and thereby reduce costs.

There are many ways to use beacons in hotels. We shall now look at how beacons can be used successfully in the hotel and in hotel catering to create customer loyalty, promote sales and track guests.

---

[112] See Schorer, Matthias: "Ubiquitous Computing ist Realität", 2016, http://www.computerwoche.de/a/ubiquitous-computing-ist-realitaet,3093580
[113] See Kamps, Ingo: "Einstieg in erfolgreiches Mobile Marketing", 2015, P. 10

The scenarios described are examples of applications, and do not claim to be the only ones:

- **Reception**

  Beacons are certain to optimize processes at reception and improve guest satisfaction. At check-in it can be seen that most of the waiting guests prefer to check out their smartphone rather than look at the hotel lobby or chat to other guests. These waiting guests can be sent messages straight to their smartphones with, for example, restaurant offers or a voucher for a free welcome drink in the hotel bar.

  But the waiting time can be further reduced. Even as guests get closer to reception, all the information required (name, address, regular guest, preferred room type, etc.) can be sent to the receptionist and appear on their display.[114] This will speed up the check-in process enormously. The guests can be greeted by name, which will make them feel valued.

  Quite possibly the principal process optimization, however, would come from automated checking-in using beacon technology. Guests are identified from Bluetooth signals as soon as they set foot in the hotel with their smartphone. The property management system is informed of their arrival,

---

[114] See Kotowski, Timo: "Einchecken ohne Hotelrezeption", 2015, http://www.faz.net/aktuell/wirtschaft/conichi-will-die-hotelrezeption-abloesen-13794028.html

rooms are assigned automatically and the digital room key is sent to the guest's smartphone so that they can go straight to their assigned room.

A beacon-assisted indoor navigation system helps the guest to find the right room using their smartphone.[115]

- **Restaurant**

  Another interesting area for using beacons is managing, and increasing use of, the hotel's restaurants or spa area.[116]

  If the hotel restaurant is under-utilized, a discount voucher or invitation to a free drink might motivate guests to visit it. Peak periods could also be spread out more if the vouchers are only valid for a certain time window (e.g. from 5pm to 7pm).

  If there is more than one restaurant, an intelligent customer load balancing system could spread the load more equally across all the restaurants, e.g. using messages or vouchers

---

[115] See Mallik, Neha: "How Hotels can use Beacons to Enhance Guest Experiences", 2014, http://blog.beaconstac.com/2014/07/how-hotels-can-use-beacons-to-enhance-guest-experiences/

[116] See Wider, Martin: "Mobile Disruption – oder warum der richtige Einsatz von Mobile für den Einzelhandel überlebenswichtig ist." in: Heinemann, Gerrit et al.: "Digitale Transformation oder digitale Disruption im Handel", 2016, P. 462-463

sent straight to the smartphone when the guest is waiting outside a restaurant that is full up.

With a better understanding of the guest, the guest can be given improved, more personalized offers which are then reflected in improved guest satisfaction and increased revenue.

A beacon could be placed beneath every table in the restaurant so that guests can be automatically navigated to a free table or their reserved table. Serving staff get a message saying who has sat down at the table and are able to greet the guests immediately using their name and with a personal recommendation. Any preferences or allergies are also picked up by servers at first contact, and can be taken into account.

If the staff are equipped with appropriate devices, e.g. with a smartwatch, they can always be in a position to respond to the guest's wishes armed with good information.

- **Spa area**

The methods used to make maximum use of the restaurant can also be applied to and implemented in the spa area. For example, cheaper treatments can be offered at short notice if utilization is temporarily low, without changing the basic price structure over the longer term.

Hotels' spa areas are often under-used or not used at all, so beacon technology could be used to draw guests' attention to the spa area if they are passing it. Here, too, taster vouchers could help arouse the guest's interest.

Personalized offerings that increase guest satisfaction can also be used in the spa area. A guest who stays at the hotel regularly and always uses the spa area but never the fitness center will not be sent any unwanted adverts for the next spinning class, but will prefer, and appreciate, a special offer in the spa area.[117]

Beacons can offer added value to those visiting the hotel's fitness center by sending information about what training machines are not being used, or sending a customized training plan to the guest's smartphone.[118]

- **Hotel room**

It is still the norm in hotels that the keycard is used to provide lighting and power. If hotels are equipped with beacons, they can automatically detect whether a guest is in the room. The guest can use the app to adjust their lighting,

---

[117] See anon.: "Zielsicher – Beacons im Hotel", 2015, https://www.onm.de/agentur/news/artikel/zielsicher-beacons-im-hotel/

[118] See Callahan, Sean: "Gyms and Fitness Centers work out better with wireless Beacons", 2016, http://www.digitalsocialretail.com/gyms-and-fitness-centers-work-out-better-with-wireless-beacons/

temperature, TV, etc. Alternatively, the beacon can automatically select the guest's preferences in terms of lighting intensity and room temperature as stored in the CRM system.[119]

If a guest, for example, returns late to the hotel and to their room, the app can advertise room service when they enter their room. A beacon message might be something like this: "Still up and about? Are you hungry? Take a look at our menu and place your food order here and now."

- **Conference area**

Beacon technology can be used to propose many appealing extra options in the hotel's conference area. When entering the conference area, delegates could be automatically checked in and get a push message to their smartphone with information about the meeting room that relates to them. At large events, the guest can be shown the number of vacant seats on their smartphone.

Other information about the conference can also be sent to guests when they are in the conference area. For example, each guest could be sent a personalized newsfeed, while

---

[119] See Callahan, Sean: "Hotels can usher in the future of hospitality by deploying innovative beacon technology", 2015, http://www.digitalsocialretail.com/hotels-can-usher-in-the-future-of-hospitality-by-deploying-innovative-beacon-technology/

large printed items such as the event program or flyers, are minimized or deleted. [120]

A practical navigation application could minimize waiting time for restrooms. With an intelligent management system, the conference delegate can, firstly, be shown where the nearest restroom is and, secondly, which of the available lavatories has the shortest waiting time. In the case of large events with short breaks, in particular, a good beacon management system offers the guest added value.

Networking is a big reason why people attend conferences. Beacons can help and be useful for networking at events. For instance, delegates can see from an app who is nearby and try to make direct contact. [121]

So beacon technology offers conference organizers new contact opportunities, greater involvement for delegates, and an improved user experience which can result in guest satisfaction being optimized.

---

[120] See Kastin, Troy: "5 ways iBeacons could make a splash in the Event Industry", 2016, http://blog.attendease.com/blog/5-ways-ibeacons-could-make-a-splash-in-the-event-industry

[121] See Sinclair, Jeff: "Proven Ways of Using Beacons to Redefine the Event Experience", 2015, http://www.eventmanagerblog.com/using-beacons-event-experience

- **Hotel buildings and grounds**

As is clear from the points above, almost all of the hotel building and the outside of the hotel can be fitted with beacons to guide the guest through the hotel and give them added value.

Should there be a safety threat (e.g. a hotel fire), beacon technology could be used to locate the hotel guests. Messages are sent to smartphones to assist in evacuation, and the indoor navigation system guides the guest safely from the hotel. Emergency services are also guided more directly to the guest.[122]

At resort hotels, the beacon at the pool area can, for example, send a message at midday saying that the restaurant is open and at the same time offering a recommendation of the day. When passing the golf course, a push message can display the green fee and possibly encourage the guest to book a golf lesson.

Similarly, business hotels benefit from outdoor beacons, by being able to send the current hotel or restaurant offers to the smartphones of passers-by.

---

[122] See Ravikumar, Rajath: "Why hotels should adopt beacon technology before it's too late", 2016, http://digitalhub.mindtree.com/why-hotels-should-adopt-beacon-technology-before-its-too-late/

3.5.3 Challenges for beacons

To fully exploit the potential of beacon technology, certain requirements from the users' perspective – i.e. from the guests' perspective – need to be taken into consideration when it comes to the actual design.[123]

To have an adequate database for improving services, the necessary data first has to be gathered. Hotels fitted with beacons can track guest behavior with precision and thus collect useful figures and data as a basis for making decisions in many application areas. For example, data gathered in the form of heat-maps can be displayed to show how many guests are where in the hotel at what time.

In this way, offerings which are particularly in demand can be identified and the hotel areas that are arousing little interest can also be picked out. Times when particularly high numbers of guests are arriving, and main meal times in the restaurant, can also be spotted.[124]

Beacons can also record how often a guest visits particular areas. In this way, a unique guest profile can be produced and the hotelier can market their services based on each guest's preferences.

---

[123] See Böpple, Oliver / Glende, Sebastian / Schauber, Cornelia: "Innovative Einkaufserlebnisse mit Beacon-Technologie gestalten" in: Linnhoff-Popien, Claudia / Zaddach, Michael / Grahl, Andreas: "Markpläzte im Umbruch – Digitale Strategien für Services im Mobilen Internet", 2015, P. 303ff.

[124] See Wächter, Mark: "Mobile Strategy", 2016, P. 109

Technology and the data collected result in a traditional customer loyalty tool with far-reaching options for identifying guests and optimizing the way they are addressed in real time. It is evident that, in the near future, hoteliers need to draw up a dedicated strategy for gathering, administering and, ultimately, using a large volume of data and information to improve their service for the guest.

Wherever user data is gathered, including via beacons, there is the issue of data protection. As the beacon only transmits its own identity, and collects no user data, it is irrelevant from a data protection perspective. For example the German data protection law, through the provisions of the Federal Data Protection Act (BDSG) and the Telemedia Act (TMG), states that personal data may only be processed with the prior consent of the person involved. Of importance, on the other hand, are the reception from the beacons on the user's device and the processing of the signals by the beacon-capable app. With the reception of the signals transmitted by the beacons, the signals are connected to the relevant user's app and, thus, connected to the personal data on the app.[125] The user needs to give their consent to the services required via the installed app. The user needs to be notified of the general terms and conditions, agree to them, and opt in. In this way, the hotel is sure that the guest has agreed to their data being used to meet their

---

[125] See Eickmeier, Frank: "Beacons & Datenschutz: Eine rechtliche Einordnung" in: eCommerce Magazine 01/2015, P. 14

101

service promise. App users are entitled to view the data that has been stored about them, and they have to be able to opt out. [126]

The app that needs to be installed and the beacon management system are the greatest challenges when using beacons:

The beacon management system provides an overview of the entire beacon landscape, as all the beacons that are installed initially are set up and inventorized there. Hotel staff should be trained to resolve any faults quickly. While live, you can use the beacon management system to check whether all the beacons are working correctly. To get the most effective use out of the beacon technology, the beacon management system needs to be connected to PMS and CRM systems. [127] These interfaces and the issue of integrating them necessitate, in turn, experienced IT personnel or service providers.

The application itself needs to be downloaded to the guest's device and installed. Many smartphone users, however, are now cautious about installing apps because they already have a great many apps

---

[126] See Jensen, Torsten / Wille, Sebastian / Wehn, Norbert: "Multisensorische Event-Erlebnisse auf Basis der iBeacon-Technologie – Bericht aus der Praxis" in: Zanger, Cornelia: "Events und Emotionen", 2015, P. 341

[127] See Kaufmann, Alexander: "Beacons: Vom Piloten zum Erfolgsprojekt" in: e-Commerce Magazin, 2015, http://www.e-commerce-magazin.de/fachartikel/beacons-vom-piloten-zum-erfolgsprojekt

installed and are focusing on using a practical number of them.[128] Any additional app needs to offer distinct added value. So in the app store there needs to be a very easily understandable description and a clear explanation of the added value. The app's design is crucial to the success of the beacon strategy. Users need to understand why the app is being installed, what data will be used and how the application will communicate with them.[129] The main challenge in designing the app is how best to integrate context-based intelligence. For, ultimately, this will be crucial in differentiating between a good and an exceptional app and, therefore, the user's willingness to download and use it.

The Bluetooth transmission technology is another technical hurdle. Around 70 percent of all smartphone owners currently have the Bluetooth function disabled on their mobile device, in order to increase their battery service life and for fear of unauthorized access.[130]

Moreover, customers will not be convinced merely by discounts and a convenient check-out if they have the feeling that they are being watched all the time. There need to be staff in the hotels who

---

[128] See anon.: "App Store Trends: Users Spend More Time in Less Apps", 2016, http://adtechdaily.com/2016/11/15/app-store-trends-users-spend-time-less-apps/

[129] See Böpple, Oliver / Glende, Sebastian / Schauber, Cornelia: "Innovative Einkaufserlebnisse mit Beacon-Technologie gestalten" in: Linnhoff-Popien, Claudia / Zaddach, Michael / Grahl, Andreas: "Markpläzte im Umbruch – Digitale Strategien für Services im Mobilen Internet", 2015, P. 303

[130] See Toedt, Michael: "Beacons – Top or Flop for the Hospitality Industry?", 2015, http://www.hospitalitynet.org/news/4073267.html

use the beacon management system prudently and only provide guests with relevant content. Ultimately, beacon technology is also a communication channel. The message to be delivered needs to include a relevant benefit for which it is worthwhile divulging more information.

3.5.4 Return on investment from beacons

The return on investment from using beacon technology can essentially be broken down into four areas: process optimization, up- and cross-selling potential, guest satisfaction and guest loyalty, and a genuine return on investment in terms of costs and the anticipated income (increased revenue).

- **Process optimization**

  The use of beacon technology has enormous potential in terms of process optimization and making work easier for hotel staff. If employees are equipped with smartphones or smartwatches, a special app can detect the location of both the customer and the member of staff. Depending on their work area, the staff member has all the relevant customer information to hand so that they can provide the best possible service.

  Housekeeping, for example, can see immediately whether there is somebody in the room and will not need to keep knocking on the door. When guests make requests, the nearest service employee can use the beacon technology to go to the guest and meet their need for an extra towel, pillow or toilet paper.[131] Reception can be notified quickly and automatically when a room has been cleaned, so that the room can be re-assigned. For analytics purposes, an application could record how long it takes to clean a room. In this way, processes can be optimized, and productivity can be measured, compared and improved.

As described previously in the section on using beacon technology at reception, there is great potential for process optimization with automated check-in (see section 3.5.2). As soon as a guest sets foot in the hotel lobby, the beacon notifies the property management system of the guest's arrival. A room is assigned automatically, the digital room key is sent to the smartphone and the hotel guest can go to their assigned room or suite.

- **Cross- und up-selling**

The real benefit of mobile technologies lies in providing relevant information at the right time and in influencing the user's behavior, as personal information is available about the guest. Using the data stored in the CRM and the beacon technology, the hotel knows who guests are, what they like, where they are right now, and what they are doing.

---

[131] See Ravikumar, Rajath: "Why hotels should adopt beacon technology before it's too late", 2016, http://digitalhub.mindtree.com/why-hotels-should-adopt-beacon-technology-before-its-too-late/

Cross- and up-selling provide opportunities to generate additional income. Well-designed mobile services offer the hotel guest increased convenience. All the relevant information is available in the given usage context. Without much effort, a smartphone can be used to reserve a table in the hotel restaurant or to set up a spa appointment. The different hotel offerings can be acquired based on the usage context, and the guest can be given incentives to purchase.

Targeted offers to smartphones can even encourage guests who prefer less personal contact (so-called silent travelers) to buy, precisely because, e.g., booking the extra service requires no further contact, but just needs a click.[132]

There is also the chance to generate additional income by advertising local companies. For example, a push message (possibly with a voucher as an incentive) can be sent for the neighborhood jeweler or the local taxi firm. The hotel then receives either a commission or a fixed payment for each message sent. This procedure is also feasible for large companies such as car rental outlets and airlines.

---

[132] See Bhakta, Vikas: "5 Tips for Attracting the Silent Traveler", 2015, https://www.bookstaygo.com/blog-for-hotels/5-tips-hotels-for-attracting-the-silent-traveler

- **Guest satisfaction and guest loyalty**

Besides the potential for up- and cross-selling, there is the opportunity to improve guest satisfaction and loyalty. The beacon technology can be used to give regular customers a special bonus depending on frequency and duration. Even as they enter the lobby, greeting messages with a voucher for a free welcome drink at the bar or a loyalty voucher for the hotel restaurant can be sent to the guest's smartphone.

Guests' satisfaction is increased by them being recognized and by their preferences being taken into account. For example, whether they like to check out late, need an extra pillow or like an allergy bed.[133] The staff on reception can provide personalized service, actively address the guest and thus create a positive guest experience.[134]

But it is not only at reception that guest satisfaction can be improved. The overall improvement in the hotel's service for the guest, throughout their stay, can also contribute to guest satisfaction and, thus, guest loyalty.

---

[133] See Richters, Kim: "Wie ein Berliner Startup den Hotelaufenthalt digitalisieren will", 2016,
http://www.gruenderszene.de/allgemein/conichi-launch-finanzierung
[134] See Warnholtz, Anna: "Und, gut geschlafen?", 2007,
https://www.welt.de/reise/article785752/Und-gut-geschlafen.html

- **Costs**

With return on investment, the issue of what investment is required is obvious. Using beacon technology is relatively cheap and the installation is inexpensive. So for a basic beacon deployment a small investment can produce a big return.[135]

A beacon generally costs between 20 and 40 euros, depending on the provider. The beacon management system is paid for by a monthly license fee. These prices vary widely, however. Providers such as Conichi charge a monthly fee on a room basis. Wingu, Onyx Beacon, Match2Blue, Barcoo (Offerista) and Sensorberg charge a monthly fee based on the amount of use.

If the beacon management system is fully integrated into the existing PMS landscape or linked to the existing CRM system, far greater spending, in terms of both time and money, is involved.

So requirements need to be identified carefully and a structured description of requirements is required in order to analyze which beacon management system provider best meets the requirements. It should be pointed out again, here, that a professional service level management system

---

[135] See Reil, Harald: "iBeacon – Apples neues Ortungssystem könnte dem stationären Handel wieder auf die Sprünge helfen" in: GENIOS WirtschaftsWissen No. 11, 2014, P. 3326

is advisable, in order to specify processes and agreements in detail and achieve agreed service levels.[136]

---

[136] See Breiter, Andreas / Fischer, Arne: "Implementierung von IT Service-Management", 2011, P. 31ff.

3.6 Virtual reality

The cultural change driven by virtual reality (VR) will be varied and widespread. The willingness to be taken away from the real world and into virtual worlds depends on personal preferences and the technical details of the VR.

This chapter will examine virtual reality (VR) opportunities for the hotel industry. As the subject is extremely current and complex, one section will deal with the history of VR. This is required because it is also used as the basis for the next section, on augmented reality.

3.6.1 History of virtual reality

Much of the background to virtual reality comes from a time well before the idea of creating virtual worlds. Stereoscopic vision, for example, was researched as far back as the 18th century. The US Air Force took the first steps towards virtual reality in the 1930s when developing the first flight simulators. However, these systems did not permit any interaction with the user.[137]

The first real VR system design was produced by Morten Heilig in 1955. But it was not until 1962 that he upgraded his idea, "The

---

[137] See Halbach, Wulf: "Interfaces: medien- und kommunikationstheoretische Elemente einer Interface-Theorie", 1994, P. 231

Cinema of the Future", to create a "Sensorama" prototype.[138] By using an integrated shaking mechanism, stereoscopic images and an odor and wind system, the user was able to experience different scenarios. However, the Sensorama remained a one-off piece, with no commercial success.[139]

In 1965, under the title "The Ultimate Display", Ivan Sutherland postulated that advances in computer technology could enable the human senses to be convinced by virtual experiences. A head-mounted display would be used here as the visual interface between man and machines. In 1968 Sutherland then developed his vision of the "Ultimate Display".[140]

The practical applications of Sutherland's displays remained restricted by the rudimentary 3D display capabilities of computer technology at that time. This technical limitation meant that in the 1960s and 1970s there were only minor advances in the virtual reality sector. Only when more high-performance graphic computers and 3D engines appeared in the 1980s and 1990s could a wide variety of applications and realistic virtual worlds be

---

[138] See Heilig, Morten: "The cinema of the future." in: Packer, Randall / Jordan, Ken: "Multimedia: From Wagner to Virtual Reality", 2002, P. 239ff.

[139] See Leinenbach, Stefan: "Interaktive Geschäftsmodellierung: Dokumentation von Prozesswissen in einer Virtual Reality-gestützten Unternehmungsvisualisierung", 2000, P. 27

[140] See Bruns, Matthias: "Virtual Reality – Eine Analyse der Schlüsseltechnologie aus der Perspektive des strategischen Managements", 2015, P. 18

displayed. In the late 1980s the entertainment industry discovered the potential of virtual reality.[141]

The commercial breakthrough for virtual reality began in 2012 with the founding of US company Oculus by Palmer Luckey. After Facebook bought the company for 2.3 billion US dollars in 2014, the Oculus Rift virtual reality headset began to be marketed commercially in 2016.[142] The same year, Sony followed with a headset for their Playstation and HTC with the Vive headset.

VR became popular and available to any user with Google's Cardboard project. For a small financial outlay modern smartphones could be transformed into simple virtual reality headsets.[143] The basic idea is easy – today's smartphones already, in principle, provide a lot of what is required to display virtual worlds. The processing power is enough for most 3D applications and integrated sensors identify directions and the end device's position. Google developed a DIY kit that enabled a simple virtual

---

[141] See Sheff, David / Eddy, Andy: "Game Over: How Nintendo Conquered the World", 1999, P. 448f.

[142] See Heinemann, Gerrit / Gaiser, Christian: "SoLoMo – Always-on im Handel: Die soziale, lokale und mobile Zukunft des Omnichannel-Shopping", 3rd edition, 2016, P. 91

[143] See anon.: "Rift, Vive, Hololense – Wie VR-Brillen 2016 das Smart Home erobern", 2016, https://www.smart-wohnen.de/virtual-reality/artikel/rift-vive-hololense-wie-vr-brillen-2016-das-smart-home-erobern/

reality headset to be made out of cardboard, Velcro fasteners and the smartphone.[144]

3.6.2 Definition of virtual reality

Virtual reality refers to a technology that, by realistically simulating sensory impressions, puts the user into a synthetically generated environment. This is referred to as immersion. The immersion is the key feature differentiating VR from other man-machine interfaces. With virtual reality, the user's sensory impressions are addressed as completely as possible by one or more output devices.[145]

For the purposes of understanding and as a basis for the content below, virtual reality may be defined as follows:

> *Virtual reality is a computer-generated, three-dimensional world that attempts to be as real as possible.*

Immersion in the computer-generated world is usually achieved using virtual reality headsets.

---

[144] See Tissler, Jan: "Google Cardboard Anleitung: Virtual Reality zum Taschengeldpreis" in: Hedemann, Falk / Tissler, Jan (ed.): "Upload Magazin 21: Virtuelle Welten", 2015, P. 60ff.
[145] See Dörner, Ralf et al. (ed.): "Virtual und Augmented Reality (VR/AR)", 2013, 13f.

3.6.3 Using virtual reality in hotels

There are many possible applications for virtual reality in hotels. We shall disregard, here, the many virtual reality options available when preparing the trip during the decision-making process (pre-stay phase), as this book does not deal with that area.

So below we shall look at the areas where virtual reality can be used in the hotel to successfully affect guest loyalty, cross- and up-selling and revenue growth. The scenarios provided are examples, and there is no suggestion that they are the only ones:

- **Hotel room**

  The hotel room will, in the future, be the place where VR is most frequently used, being an extension of the hotel's room service.

  In the future, instead of the TV, hotel guests will be able to use a virtual reality headset and immerse themselves in the hotel's range of pay films or become part of a video game. Erotic offerings will be a particular driver of virtual reality here, and enable hotels to increase revenues from pay TV.[146]

---

[146] See anon.: "Hotels bieten eigene VR-Brillen für Pornografie an", 2016, http://www.gulli.com/news/27379-hotels-bieten-eigene-vr-brillen-fuer-pornografie-an-2016-04-21

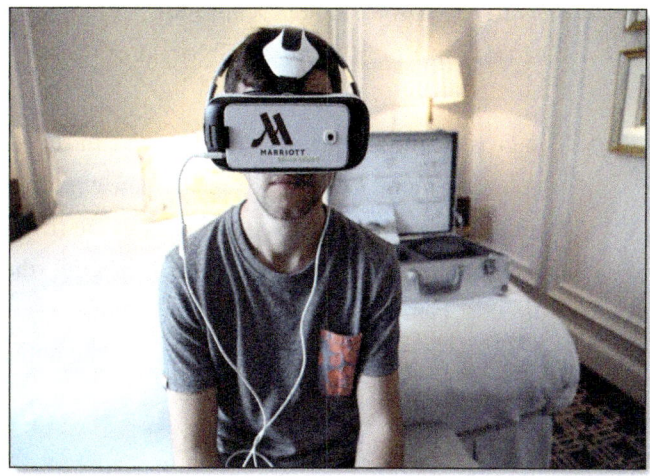

Fig. 10: "Example of a VR headset in the hotel room"
Source: Engadget.com, 2015

Guests can also be offered virtual immersion in fantasy worlds, such as space, or a land with dragons, in their hotel room. In this respect, the headset can add to the experience at the vacation spot and make it even more memorable.

Sightseeing, too, can be done from the hotel room first. In this way, guests can decide beforehand whether the sight is worth visiting.

Business travelers could enjoy using the VR headset to move from their small room in New York to a beach in

115

Hawaii. Marriott Hotels calls this offering a "virtual postcard" and use it to cross-sell for other Marriott hotels.[147]

The cross-selling aspect of VR headsets in the hotel room is relevant more generally. Guests can explore the hotel from their room, and take a prior look at the restaurant, spa or fitness area in the hotel. Experiencing these areas indirectly can increase the probability of a real visit and thus result in the guest spending more in the hotel.

- **Spa and fitness area**

In the fitness area, VR headsets offer the opportunity of a completely new experience. Instead of monotonously viewing the latest news on a TV from the treadmill, guests with VR headsets can jog through an imaginary forest. Or take part in a race between Oxford and Cambridge, the famous English universities, on the rowing machine. Competing virtually in the Tour de France or Giro D'Italia are also possible.[148] This could be a whole new motivation.

It could also be that hotels add VR experience areas to their fitness area. So that guests can, for example fight an

---

[147] See anon.: "Marriott Hotels Introduces The First Ever In-Room Virtual Reality Travel Experience", 2015, http://news.marriott.com/2015/09/marriott-hotels-introduces-the-first-ever-in-room-virtual-reality-travel-experience/

[148] See Kühl, Eike: "Auf dem Heimtrainer durchs schwarze Loch", 2016, http://www.zeit.de/digital/internet/2016-08/virtual-reality-fitness-radfahren-google-street-view

imaginary dragon in a fantasy world. Or that in this area guests can book a virtual tennis hour with Andre Agassi or Roger Federer as their trainer.

The combination of sport and adventure can be an additional source of income for hotels, help improve guest satisfaction and provide a competitive advantage.

In the spa area, lying on the sun-bench can be made more pleasant by the guest using a VR headset. As well as the warmth from the sunlamp, guests can be immersed in a virtual scenario on the beach.

- **Reception and lobby**

When guests check in at reception, they can be given the option to, for example, sample high-priced suites. This could encourage the guest to book a higher category room.

VR headsets could be laid out in the lobby and guests could sample, virtually, other hotels of the same brand in other destinations. This would also help to make things more pleasant if check-in waiting times are lengthy.

- **Conference area**

Virtual reality technology can significantly change the banqueting and event area. Room designs and seating plans will be superseded by VR headsets so that meeting plans can be optimized. Potential conference organizers can use VR headsets to study each room with any seating arrangement.

The room can also be populated with virtual people to get an impression of the event's atmosphere. Visual sales presentations can directly match the organizers' ideas and expectations.

Generally speaking, it should be pointed out that virtual reality currently only exists in a few hotels. It may be assumed that over the coming years more hotels will offer this service and come up with other types of application, and that the digital guest experience in the hotel will be extended.

3.6.4 Challenges for virtual reality

The biggest challenge for virtual reality is currently still so-called motion sickness, also referred to as virtual reality sickness, simulator sickness and cyber sickness. Motion sickness is also known as sea sickness and travel sickness, and academically it is called kinetosis. This sickness still occurs very frequently and very rapidly when people are immersed in virtual worlds using VR headsets. Kinetosis is caused by stress hormones that the body discharges when the visual experience fails to match other perceptions. [149] The organ of equilibrium senses a dissonance

---

[149] See Pose, Ronald / Regan, Matthew: "Techniques for Reducing Virtual Reality Latency with Architectural Support and Consideration

between what the eyes are recording and the actual movement. The results can include nausea, dizziness, headaches and generally feeling unwell.[150]

The long-term effects of immersion in virtual worlds is not yet sufficiently well known. There is an urgent need to carry out further research, but this can only be effective to a limited degree, because children and people with pre-existing conditions are not studied for ethical reasons. However, it is these people in particular who can be especially easy to influence. Researchers at Johannes Gutenberg University Mainz have found that immersion in a virtual reality can cause behavioral changes which continue to endure when the person has left the VR environment.[151] In this context, both users and content producers are responsible for which VR content they allow themselves and others.[152]

Up to now, another limiting factor with virtual reality has been a lack of feel. Immersion in virtual worlds is currently still limited to

---

of Human Factors" in: Brusilovski, Peter / Kommers, Piet: "Multimedia, Hypermedia and Virtual Reality", 1994, P. 117

[150] See Kolasinski, Eugenia: "Simulator Sickness in Virtual Environments", 1995, P. 10

[151] See Madary, Michael / Metzinger, Thomas: "Real Virtuality: A Code of Ethical Conduct. Recommendations for Good Scientific Practice and the Consumers of VR-Technology", 2016, http://journal.frontiersin.org/article/10.3389/frobt.2016.00003/full

[152] On this, see also Bente, Gary et al.: "Virtuelle Realität als Gegenstand und Methode in der Psychologie" in: Bente, Gary et al. (ed.): "Virtuelle Realitäten", 2002, P. 1

visual, aural and a reduced range of movement.[153] The immersion quality suffers as a result. As realistic as the graphics in a virtual reality headset will one day be, as long as nothing can be touched in the virtual world the limits will always be clearly defined.

In relation to virtual reality, little attention is paid to the issue of data protection. But virtual reality systems can give rise to new opportunities to collect data, e.g. emotions, eye movements and body movements. The data gathered can then be used in targeted marketing measures. With the use of the Oculus Rift VR headset, in particular, it should be pointed out that Oculus belongs to Facebook and existing user profiles can be enriched from virtual reality use. VR system users need to be told which data they are divulging, which data will be collected and for what purposes it will be used.[154]

3.6.5 Return on investment of virtual reality

Hotels that wish to present their own content using a virtual reality application face other challenges in terms of time and money. Depending on the nature and scope of a virtual reality experience, the project will take between two weeks and several months. The

---

[153] See Heger, Rainer: "Entwicklung eines Systems zur interaktiven Gestaltung und Auswertung von manuellen Montagetätigkeiten in der virtuellen Realität.", 1998, P. 134

[154] See Müller, Andreas: "Oculus Rift & Datenschutz: Diese Daten sammelt die VR-Brille", 2016, https://www.turn-on.de/play/ratgeber/oculus-rift-datenschutz-diese-daten-sammelt-die-vr-brille-76739

cost starts at around 20,000 euros.[155] Even though some hotels and hotel groups are already using VR to generate additional revenue there is, as yet, no documentary evidence from either the room upselling or event sales areas.

The cost of a VR headset ranges from 300 to 800 euros. Bearing in mind the potential increase in guest satisfaction and an advantage vis-à-vis the competition, hotels ought to begin to equip at least some of their rooms with VR systems. The use of the VR headsets can then be an additional source of income. After all, guests do not need to be given free access to 3D films or games, but rather they can be billed, as is the case with Pay TV.

It should also be pointed out that over the coming years there will be a major step-up in the quality of headsets from current models to the next generation. Headset display quality will continue to improve and the differences between reality and virtuality will become increasingly blurred. The headsets will also keep getting cheaper, smaller, lighter and more convenient and they will find their way into more and more hotel rooms. In general, therefore, the question for hotels is when the right time is to move into virtual reality in order, on the one hand, to not be burdened with big investments while, on the other, being able to profit from virtual reality at an early stage.

---

[155] See Kleingers, Sarah: "Was kostet die virtuelle Welt", 2016, https://recordbay.de/virtual-reality-kosten/

3.7 Augmented reality

Augmented reality (AR) is a logical step-up from virtual reality (VR). In contrast to VR, in AR the actual reality surrounding the user is enriched by three-dimensional virtual elements. While the user is sealed off from the outside world with VR headsets, so that what they experience appears as real as possible, AR is seamlessly embedded into the environment in real time. New objects are displayed or additional information is provided about existing objects in direct spatial relationship.[156] In contrast to virtual reality, no new worlds are created, but the existing reality is enriched through a virtual reality.

3.7.1 Definition of augmented reality

There is, as yet, no standard definition of augmented reality in the literature. The reality-virtuality continuum developed by Milgram et al. is often referenced. This postulates a continuous transition between the real and virtual environment.[157]

The left part of the continuum describes environments solely comprising real objects. The right-hand side, on the other hand, defines environments that only consist of virtual objects. Within this framework, mixed reality is defined as an environment in which

---

[156] See Tönnis, Marcus: "Augmented Reality – Einblicke in die Erweiterte Realität", 2010, P. I

[157] See Milgram, Paul et al.: "Augmented Reality: A class of displays on the reality-virtuality continuum" in: SPIE: "Telemanipulator and Telepresence Technologies", Issue 2351, 1994, P. 283

real and virtual objects are combined at will in a display.[158] With augmented reality it is the reality that predominates.

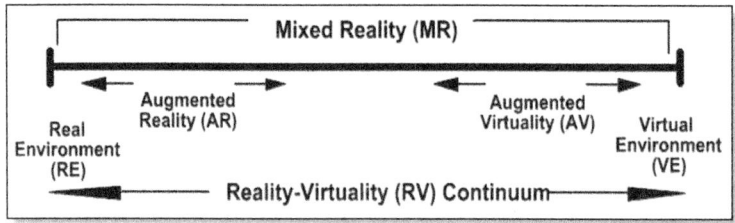

Fig. 11: "Reality-Virtuality Continuum"
Source: Drhu.eu, 2012

On this basis, in this book augmented reality should be understood and defined as follows:

> *Augmented reality refers to a computer-based display that enriches the real world with virtual aspects.*

It should be pointed out here that the following conditions need to be in place with augmented reality: augmented reality must combine the real and the virtual, the interaction must occur in real

---

[158] See Mehler-Bicher, Anett / Steiger, Lothar: "Augmented Reality: Theorie und Praxis", 2nd revised edition, 2014, P.10

time, and there has to be a three-dimensional relationship of virtual and real objects.[159]

3.7.2 Types of augmented reality

Augmented reality occurs particularly using mobile devices such as tablets and smartphones. Using an augmented reality app, the smartphone camera and, possibly, the integrated GPS, the user uses the device display to see the real environment enriched by virtual objects. One should distinguish between the following types of applied augmented reality.[160]

- **Location-based augmented reality**

  With this variant, the identifying of the location triggers the AR projection. The Global Positioning System (GPS) satellite technology detects the location. The viewing direction and inclination of the smartphone also feed into the calculation via the integrated hardware components such as the compass and movement sensors. The AR app overlays relevant data on top of a real view, in the right position.

---

[159] See Azuma, Ronald: "A Survey of Augmented Reality" in: "Presence: Teleoperators and Virtual Enviroments" 1997, P 356

[160] See Chaplais, Christian: "What Augmented Reality Can Bring to the Industry and Why it Will Take Time", 2016, http://www.apriso.com/blog/2016/11/what-augmented-reality-can-bring-to-the-industry-and-why-it-will-take-time/

- **Marker-based augmented reality**

This type of augmented reality uses custom patterns or images. The so-called markers are usually just QR code but they may also be predefined image elements in a catalog. The AR application uses image recognition to identify them so that the associated content can be assigned and displayed. The three-dimensionality of the display is created by the perspectives and positioning of the marker.[161]

- **Marker-less augmented reality**

With image recognition software that runs with ever greater precision, architectural structures can be recognized.[162] Software-based face recognition itself is well advanced, so that augmentations can be registered on the physiognomy of a face. For augmented reality, this means that optical markers will soon no longer be needed. The processing power of mobile devices is constantly increasing, and image recognition software is becoming better at

---

[161] See Brendel, Nadine: "(Mobile) Augmented Reality – Hype oder nachhaltiges Marketinginstrument?", 2011, http://www.marketing-boerse.de/Fachartikel/details/Mobile-Augmented-Reality-%96-Hype-oder-nachhaltiges-Marketinginstrument/33276

[162] See Azuma, Ronald: "Overview of Augmented Reality", in: Siggraph 2004: "Proceedings of the Conference on Siggraph 2004 course notes", 2004, P. 26

recognizing the 3D structures in a space and, thus, being able to register augmentations on it.[163]

- **Enterprise augmented reality**

  The enterprise solution of augmented reality applications is used mainly in factories. AR is incorporated into the company's value added chain and aims to help optimize processes.

3.7.3 Using augmented reality in hotels

There are a number of possibilities for using augmented reality in hotels. Some applications will be described below. We shall look at how augmented reality can help increase guest satisfaction, increase sales and grow revenue when used with hotel bookings, in the hotel itself and in the hotel's catering service.

- **Hotel searches**

  A smartphone is used to show potential guests which direction they need to go to find the nearest hotel.

---

[163] See Licht, Lucas: "Augmented and Mixed Reality – Die Welt als Hyperlink" 2010, P, 25

Fig. 12: "Example of an AR hotel search"
Source: Augmented Reality Trends, 2013

To minimize the app installation barrier, Microsoft has added an augmented reality function to its Bing search for Android, to help users search for nearby cafés, restaurants and hotels.[164] Google will undoubtedly follow suit before long, and using augmented reality to search for hotels will become more common.

---

[164] See Bordel, Stefan: "Microsoft rüstet Bing-Suche mit Augmented Reality auf", 2016,
http://www.internetworld.de/onlinemarketing/microsoft/microsoft-ruestet-bing-suche-augmented-reality-1152870.html

- **Hotel bookings**

Ideally, the AR application will display the "From" price for a room in the hotel concerned, and the guest will be able to book the hotel using the application on their mobile.

If potential guests point their smartphone at the hotel building, they can be shown the hotel's cheapest rates and availability. The guest then enters the booking process and makes their booking.

In the future, potential guests could also be able to stand right in front of a hotel and see from their smartphone display which rooms are available in the hotel. For example, the guest can see whether, e.g. a room is free on the top floor of the hotel, and book it straight away. This presupposes a digital room assignment system, as described in section 3.1.3.

- **Hotel check-in**

When the technology as a whole is more advanced, receptionists can be equipped with a Google Glass and use face recognition to see who is in front of them wanting to check in. [165] The glasses either give the employee information from the social web or from the hotel's own

---

[165] See McGee, Matt: "Social Media Via Google Glass: Florida Agency Has An App For That", 2014, http://marketingland.com/social-media-via-google-glass-florida-agency-app-78218

CRM database, so that they can address the guest personally and satisfy their particular needs.

Fig. 13: "Hotel receptionist with a Google Glass"
Source: Marketingland.com, 2015

Some independent hotels in the USA (e.g. the b2 Miami Downtown hotel) have already begun to issue the Google Glass to their front-desk staff and make use of social media potential.[166]

---

[166] See Levy, Karyne: "The Concierge At This Fancy San Francisco Hotel Uses Google Glass", 2014,
http://www.businessinsider.com/the-concierge-at-this-fancy-san-francisco-hotel-uses-google-glass-2014-4?IR=T

- **Hotel advertising**

In the future, hotels will be able to distribute flyers or catalogs of their services (e.g. offers in the hotel restaurant or spa area) and potential guests will use augmented reality to get more information on their smartphone or tablet. The much-postulated but little-used QR code will, then, gradually vanish from the communication.[167]

- **Hotel indoor navigation**

When guests have been assigned their room, they can use their smartphone to follow a virtual butler. The butler will appear in the device's display and take the guest to the room, so the guest is guided through the hotel. Less expensively, virtual arrows on the smartphone can also navigate the guest to their room.[168] (See Figure 14)

---

[167] See Borison, Rebecca: "Marriott Hotels reimagines travel with augmented reality", 2013, http://www.mobilemarketer.com/cms/news/software-technology/16391.html

[168] See Chang, Christina: "Augmented Reality Applications in the Tourism Industry", 2016, http://www.augment.com/blog/augmented-reality-in-tourism/

Fig. 14: "Example of indoor navigation"
Source: Staywyse.org, 2015

Indoor navigation can also be used to find the spa area or be guided to the hotel restaurant.

Augmented reality can also provide useful help if there is an evacuation, and guide the guest to the nearest emergency exit.

- **Hotel room**

In their hotel room, the guest can use augmented reality via their smartphone to be shown where the nearest unused power socket, or master switch for the lighting, is. Guests can also have the air-conditioning system explained to them (which can be of genuine added value to foreign guests in particular).[169] Google has had, since 2015, a feature in its translation app for smartphones which is aimed at making it easier for users to get help while traveling in countries where foreign languages are spoken. Text captured using the mobile phone's camera is translated in real time and there is an attempt to retain the original font style. The translation feature can also be installed on a digital concierge table (as in section 3.4) and be available as an add-on service.

The augmented reality translation scenario is useful for throughout the hotel building.

There is an additional source of income to be had if the guest uses an AR app to get commercial information about the inventory in the hotel room. For instance, guests could see the price of the bedding displayed and then order it, straight away, online, so that they can sleep as comfortably at home as they do in the hotel.

- **Hotel restaurant**

When visiting the restaurant, augmented reality can provide valuable additional information about the wine that has been served. Or the guest can be shown how many calories their food has or precisely what ingredients are in the meal.

---

[169] See Radde, Björn: "Virtual und Augmented Reality", 2014, http://www.page-consulting.de/allgemein/virtual-und-augmented-reality/

If any allergies have been entered in the CRM system, a warning can appear. Similarly, vegans can find out whether their menu is really free of animal products.

Fig. 15: "Displaying additional information"
Source: Foodpix.co, 2016

It is also possible that augmented reality can be used to display the menu in three dimensions. The guest can then see on their smartphone how the dish would look.[170]

The ratings system for restaurants and hotel services, familiar from eCommerce, can be broken down to individual dishes. The guest would use the augmented

---

[170] See Allen, Aaron: "Restaurant Marketing Ideas: 10 Examples of Augmented Reality", 2016, http://aaronallen.com/blog/restaurant-marketing/augmented-reality

reality app to view ratings given by other guests for the dish concerned.

- **Meeting and conference area**

Augmented reality can guide conference delegates to the right room and, possibly, to the restroom (see Indoor navigation). And event organizers can provide further information about the speaker on the stage via an augmented reality app.[171] If there were an exhibition in the hotel, real objects could be displayed which, due to their sheer size or complexity, cannot be exhibited live, and visitors could even interact with them.[172]

- **Hotel boutique**

In hotel boutiques, augmented reality in the form of so-called living mirrors can be used. The guest stands in front of an over-sized display, the augmented reality system recognizes the face or body of the viewer and accurately positions three-dimensional objects on the head or body. The guest thus sees themselves on the display with an item of clothing without really having to try it on.[173] It is also feasible that the artificial mirror displays other information

---

[171] Funk, Christian: "Digitalisation is key" in: CIM – Conference & Incentive Management, Special GBB, 2015, P. 40f.

[172] See Mehler-Bicher, Anett / Steiger, Lothar: "Augmented Reality: Theorie und Praxis", 2nd revised edition, 2014, P. 23

[173] ibid, P. 23

(for example, the material, care instructions or price) about the article of clothing.

All the augmented reality scenarios mentioned already exist in the hotel sector or are being developed. How many of the technological possibilities will be successful in the long term remains to be seen.

3.7.4 Challenges for augmented reality

As with many guest experience tools, the content and how guests will use AR presents a challenge. Before programming begins there needs to be a design phase to take detailed decisions about the content and functions that the augmented reality solution (e.g. in the form of a mobile app) should have.

When creating an augmented reality solution there are two options: the hotel can either create its own native app or use augmented reality browsers. The choice depends largely on the functions that are to be provided. AR browsers often only provide a limited number of potential features. Designing native apps means integrating the AR technology directly into an app. The complexity is increased if hotels already have their own hotel app and want to enrich it with the features of augmented reality options.

Once the app has been programmed, it has to be downloaded onto the guest's device. Native apps are often over 100MB in size and that volume of data is rarely downloaded while traveling. If the app is installed on the guest's device, there can still be barriers to a top-quality guest experience. If the lighting is poor, or if a marker is covered, the augmented reality application will not respond and the guest will be disappointed. With GPS-based applications, the positioning technology may not work well indoors or in closed rooms with no reception, though solutions may now be in the pipeline.[174]

Ethical issues are a big challenge. The social aspects of augmented reality are just as important as the technological aspects. At the moment, it is difficult to predict how society will react to the possibilities of augmented reality. From a data protection perspective, personal identification in real time using augmented reality can pose a real threat. As stated, AR applications can match a person to data from social networks. Not only through details which indicate who the person is, but other information too, such as preferences, that can enable a targeted marketed measure. If the person identified has not explicitly agreed to their being identified and addressed with marketing measures, there is a data protection problem.[175]

3.7.5 Return on investment from augmented reality

It is relatively difficult to assess the return on investment from augmented reality, as many of the applications described generate

---

[174] See Auel, Kersten: "Personal Indoor Assistant: Den richtigen Weg finden mit Augmented Reality", 2015, https://www.heise.de/ix/meldung/Personal-Indoor-Assistant-Den-richtigen-Weg-finden-mit-Augmented-Reality-2655997.html
[175] See Lobe, Adrian: "Die Welt durch die Brille der Softwarekonzerne", 2014, http://www.tagesspiegel.de/medien/augmented-reality-die-welt-durch-die-brille-der-softwarekonzerne/11114582.html

no direct financial impacts. This raises the question as to which criteria may be useful for assessment purposes. It should be pointed out that the benefits are not purely objective, i.e. they cannot be expressed in figures and data. Rather, it is important to assess the benefits that using augmented reality offer the guest, and to what degree these benefits meet the user's needs for information and entertainment.[176]

Consequently, we shall assess the application areas based on guest satisfaction and potential competitive advantage, and make certain assumptions about a monetary effect.

- **Guest satisfaction**

  Augmented reality substantially improves guest satisfaction at check-in, with indoor navigation and by translating to their own language. Guests are spared lengthy processes and the unpleasant feeling of being unable to read, or understand, foreign text. Using augmented reality, guests can experience a completely new type of access to the hotel's services and the hotel itself. If the guest, in the restaurant, knows what ingredients are in their menu and whether they are in harmony with their eating habits, this impacts on their satisfaction. Ultimately, augmented reality is just fun, something which, again, has a positive effect on the guest's satisfaction.

---

[176] See Müller, Mirjam: "Augmented Reality in der Praxis", 2011, http://heftarchiv.internetworld.de/2011/Ausgabe-21-2011/Augmented-Reality-in-der-Praxis.

- **Competitive advantage**

  The interactivity associated with AR technology not only enables the hotel to be experienced through multiple senses, but also has a positive effect on its memorability. This positive memory may encourage the guest to return and constitute a competitive advantage.

  Another competitive advantage is the image that the hotel presents. An innovative hotel that uses augmented reality technology is giving a signal that it can satisfy guests' technological requirements.[177]

- **Costs**

  There are two ways to produce an augmented reality solution. Either a native app can be created or hotels can use augmented reality browsers. The choice depends largely on the hotel's needs. It is difficult to make a satisfactory, cut-and-dried statement. Prices can vary from between 1,000 to 500,000 euros. As with the deployment of any digital guest experience tool described in this book, the requirements and objectives need to be carefully analyzed and documented.

---

[177] See Mandelbaum, Abi: "How hotels could use augmented reality", 2015, https://ehotelier.com/insights/2015/07/21/how-hotels-could-use-augmented-reality/

There are further cost savings from hotel staff and staff in the hotel restaurant needing to provide less information. An augmented reality application can answer many of the guests' questions beforehand.

- **Increased revenue**

An increase in revenue may be anticipated in any area where augmented reality is used. Cross- and up-selling often fails with guests due to a lack of information. If services can be enriched with additional information, the guest may be won over and revenue increased. As with online shopping, other guests' ratings can prompt people to book an add-on service.[178]

If the front-desk agent or the restaurant employee has additional information about the guest, they can cater for the guest's potential wishes in an immediate (real time), targeted way, thus generating more income.

- **Process optimization**

Besides the process optimization for front-desk agents also the cleaning staff can benefit from augmented reality solutions. The staff can get computer-based instructions via their glasses that include which tasks should be completed, when, where and how.

---

[178] See Wolf, Isabella: "Augmented Reality am Point of Sale", 2016, http://www.marketmentor.org/de/augmented-reality-point-sale/

The staff will know in what order to clean a room, what tools and cleaning agents to use, and whether they are using enough pressure on the tools to achieve the desired results. That means fewer mistakes and down-time, better quality work, on-the-spot training and a process optimization.[179]

To summarize, it should be pointed out that only useful applications which are beneficial to the hotel guest will be a crucial factor for the success of augmented reality and a positive return on investment.

---

[179] anon.: "Augmented reality start-up aims for cleaner rooms", 2017, http://ehotelier.com/global/2017/03/22/augmented-reality-startup-aims-cleaner-rooms/

3.8 Voicebots, Chatbots and conversational commerce

Facebook has "M", Amazon has "Alexa", Apple has developed both "Viv" and "Siri", IBM have their "Watson", Google have announced their "Allo" assistant service and Samsung unveils "Bixby". There are also some travel-specific chatbots such as "Lola" and "Pana".

Conversational commerce using bots and messaging systems is a hot topic in the current debate about the mega-trends of the coming years, and it is already being dubbed a 'game changer' for eCommerce.[180] These are primarily new communication interfaces which are the next logical, evolutionary stage, providing benefits in terms of efficiency and convenience. Bot development is due to lead to fundamentally different principles in communication and the relevant interfaces.[181]

Chatbots will replace many current websites and apps. Bots annul the separation of application-based functions. For instance, one transaction can include the evaluation of a product, the choice, the purchase and the service. Historically, a consumer would need to use different apps or websites to achieve this. So the chatbot is used

---

[180] See Castanon, Raul: "Conversational technologies will be a key game changer in 2017", 2016, https://chatbotslife.com/conversational-technologies-will-be-a-key-game-changer-in-2017-18ca0555553c#.l62dpx7dq
[181] See Maire, Ludovic: "Conversational commerce is about to revolutionize retail", 2016, https://www.valtech.com/blog/conversational-commerce-is-about-to-revolutionize-retail/

as a generic platform and combines the different types of information and transaction into one continuous transaction. Based on learned preferences, the bot can make a choice, trigger the order and finalize the transaction using known bank and address details.[182]

3.8.1 Definition of chatbots

In 1966, the German-American computer scientist Joseph Weizenbaum created Eliza, the mother of all chatbots. A computer program that answers the user's inputs in as human a manner as possible. Countless bots have been developed since Eliza. Every year, in the Loebner Prize process, IT experts and researchers test subjects. The researchers aim to find out which bot most closely matches a genuine conversational partner. The results are not always convincing.

Bots became more complex with the World Wide Web. In 2001 AOL's AIM, the leading messenger at that time, launched the SmarterChild bot which was not only able to answer, but also provide information about the weather, news and cinema listings.[183] In many respects SmarterChild was the predecessor to bots such as

---

[182] See Gentsch, Peter: "Digitale Transformation im E-Business: Conversational Commerce als Game Changer", 2016, https://www.xing.com/communities/posts/digitale-transformation-im-e-business-conversational-commerce-als-game-changer-1012440284

[183] See Kühl, Eicke: "Hey, du Mensch!", 2016, http://www.zeit.de/digital/internet/2016-04/facebook-messenger-chatbots-zukunft

Poncho, but also to virtual assistants such as Apple's Siri and Microsoft's Cortana.

Fig. 16: "Amazon Echo with voicebot Alexa"
Source: N-TV, 2016

Today's chatbots can take complete control over an account or profile on a messenger or social media app and respond automatically to direct text commands. They generate their custom replies by asking their chat partner questions, analyzing keywords, and processing sentences from natural conversations. They are intelligent to varying degrees.

We are currently finding that most chatbots work based on scripts. This means that there is a defined set of keywords, questions, replies and subjects. The input that the chatbot receives makes it more intelligent over time. Many companies are currently playing it safe by using these scripted bots.[184]

For further understanding within this book, we have defined chatbots as follows:

> *A chatbot is a technology with artificial intelligence that can hold conversations with human users.*

3.8.2 Using voicebots and chatbots in hotels

In the future, conversational commerce and chatbots will most commonly be used to book hotel rooms. But there are also ways in which they can be used in the hotel itself to positively impact the digital guest experience. The following possibilities are plausible, though they are not claimed to be the only ones:

- **Room service**

  In the hotel room chatbots or voicebot can submit simple food and drink orders. By means of a simple voice instruction the guest can, for example, order a club sandwich and a cola. The bot can also recommend a dessert, actively driving up-selling in the process.

---

[184] See Wray, Evan: "5 Dinge, die Unternehmen über Chatbots wissen sollten" in: InternetWorld Business, 2016, http://www.internetworld.de/technik/bots/5-dinge-unternehmen-chatbots-wissen-1134601.html

Other services, such as ironing, laundry and shoe-shine, can also be ordered directly using the chatbot. Unlike concierge tablet applications, the bot can possibly ask what time the service is required.

In principle, all the technology in the room could be controlled by voicebot systems. One can imagine, for instance, the lighting being switched on or dimmed using voice commands. The climate control system can be set to a particular temperature with a simple voice instruction, or the drapes opened. The TV can also be controlled using a chatbot system.

- **Restaurant visits**

Hotel guests can use chatbot systems to reserve a table in the restaurant. Here, too, the bot can ask questions about the number of people or the required time. The bot system might be able to suggest an alternative time if the restaurant is already quite busy.[185]

- **Spa treatments**

As with the restaurant's offerings, it should also be possible to reserve the hotel's spa options using chatbots. Hotel guests are often reluctant to visit the hotel spa because, for

---

[185] See Jackson, John: "Using a chatbot to start a conversation with restaurant regulars", 2016, http://venturebeat.com/2016/10/06/using-a-chatbot-to-start-a-conversation-with-restaurant-regulars/

one thing, they do not know where it is, or they fear that there will be no treatment windows available during their stay, or they think that a treatment is too expensive. The bot can, in a conversation, eliminate these concerns and thereby increase use of the hotel's spa.

- **Destination information and sightseeing tours**

Chat systems are particularly well-suited to answering questions. So it could be that bots are able to answer specific queries about destinations – where a particular monument is, how far it is to the airport, etc. The bots could then be used to order the appropriate service such as a taxi or a sightseeing tour.

If a sightseeing tour is booked via the chatbot system, the hotel receives an appropriate commission from the provider.

- **Hotel stays**

Hotel guests can conveniently use the chatbot from their hotel room to book their next stay. In the future, it may also be that special rates are only available via the chatbot system in the room, so that the guest gets a certain price benefit by making the booking. It would be ideal if guests can tell the bot that they want to re-book precisely that room where they currently are.[186]

As chatbot systems are not yet being widely used, there are no reliable findings yet, and no case study with sound results concerning increased revenue.

In Las Vegas, Wynn is the first hotel to have installed an Amazon Alexa chatbot system in all their rooms. It may be assumed that initial successful results will be announced before long.[187]

3.8.3 Challenges for voicebots and chatbots

In contrast to most of the digital experience tools described in this book, with voicebots a challenge is that it is unusual for guests to speak to a machine (as with the use of service robots as described in section 3.2). Hotel guests tend to want to talk to, and be understood by, a real person, particularly when it comes to complicated issues such as a complaint.

For guests it can also be strange that there is a device within their intimate space in the hotel room that can listen in to every conversation or sound. For users it is not sufficiently clear how, to what extent and where the information gathered will be processed.

---

[186] On this, see 3.1 "Digital Room Assignment"
[187] See Balakrishnan, Anita: "Wynn Las Vegas to add Amazon Alexa to all hotel rooms", 2016, http://www.cnbc.com/2016/12/14/wynn-las-vegas-to-add-amazon-alexa-to-all-hotel-rooms.html

Neither is it clear for how long the data will be stored.[188] In this context, hotels are called upon to not abuse the technology and to protect their guests' private sphere.

The voicebots' speech quality can also be a challenge. If a guest has the feeling that he would be talking to a simple machine, it can have a negative impact on the guest experience. The effect can be similarly negative if the questions asked are not understood. But machines will always face the challenge of understanding people correctly. For even people, when talking to one another, are not always able to properly clarify the sense and the intention behind what they say.[189]

Speech recognition for foreign guests is another challenge, particularly for the hotel industry. Up to now, voicebots and chatbots have only each mastered one language. Hotels with many international guests need to be conscious of them, even though an improvement can be anticipated in the near future in this respect, since the technology for more than one language already exists.

The many users in the hotel may also pose a challenge for the bots' artificial intelligence. The systems learn, at times, to adjust to their users' needs (intent recognition). When hotel guests are constantly

---

[188] See Wilkens, Andreas: "Datenschutzbeauftrage Voßhoff warnt vor Amazon Echo", 2016,
https://www.heise.de/newsticker/meldung/Datenschutzbeauftragte-Vosshoff-warnt-vor-Amazon-Echo-3380364.html

[189] See Fedossov, Alexander: "Was sind Chatbots und wo sind ihre Grenzen?", 2016, https://wollmilchsau.de/personalmarketing/wer-oder-was-sind-chatbots/

changing, the "learning" can be negatively affected and even useless.

The biggest challenge lies in interlinking the chatbot system with other hotel systems. If a guest uses the bot to reserve a table in the hotel restaurant, the reservation also needs to get into the restaurant's system.[190] The same applies to room service and the CRM system.

3.8.4 Return on investment of chatbots

The hardware costs for putting chatbot systems into the hotel room have become quite low. An Amazon Echo device with the Alexa chatbot is already available for under 200 euros. Configuring the chatbot to the hotel's needs and the existing hotel systems requires a greater financial outlay.

The return on this investment can be achieved in the following areas:

- **Increased revenue**

  The potential uses of chatbot systems in the hotel, as described above, are mainly aimed at generating additional revenue from room service, the spa area and the hotel restaurant.

---

[190] See Braun, Alexander: "Chatbots in der Kundenkommunikation", 2003, P. 38

▪ **Cost reduction**

Guests can access chatbot systems around the clock. This means that they can take over the role of a concierge and save that cost point.

▪ **Improved guest satisfaction**

Guest satisfaction can be increased by chatbot systems, as the guest can use the system at any time and have their questions answered. Voice-controlled systems also offer a benefit to people with impaired vision. Apart from the capability to control the room's features, restaurant tables and spa treatments can be booked verbally, as has been described. There is no longer a need to dial a phone number, as the systems work using activation words (e.g. "Alexa!", "Siri!").

Voicebot systems might also be fitted with so-called service tone analyzers.[191] These enable spoken texts to be analyzed, and they infer the speaker's mood from words and the pitch. The chatbot system can then suggest things to the guest that will improve their mood (e.g. a visit to the spa, or a particular film on Pay TV).

---

[191] See Gielnik, Nina-Franziska: "Robots powered by IBM Watson erobern die Hotellerie: ein personalisiertes Hotelerlebnis mit Concierge Connie", 2016, https://cloudikon.de/robots-powered-by-ibm-watson-erobern-die-hotellerie/

Chatbot systems can be used to get guest feedback via direct, private chats. In the enclosed, quiet atmosphere of the hotel room, the guest might be encouraged to answer specific questions about their experience with the hotel.

All in all, an increasingly data-driven, analytical hotel business will need to answer the question about the right balance between automation and personal interaction. It remains to be seen how common chatbot systems and conversational commerce will become. The implications for the guest are equally enthralling.

3.9 Mobile apps

With the Internet and the invention of smartphones, unrestricted mobility has been achieved through personal accessibility and independence of location.[192] So tourism and the hotel industry are ideal for using mobile devices, because the travel sector not only compels sensitivity of information, but also flexibility in terms of location.[193] The positive advance of technology in the mobile phone market and personalization in the tourism sector go hand in hand, so that the mobile device can be used in every phase of tourist value creation.

As the preceding sections have made clear, most digital guest experience tools require the guest to install a mobile app. To this extent, an app which works well and is tailored to the user is sometimes a prerequisite for the positive guest experience in terms of digital guest experience management tools.

3.9.1 Definition of mobile apps

"App" is the abbreviation for the word "application". As this very general term suggests, it can cover a wide variety of different software programs. In contrast to desktop applications, mobile apps

---

[192] See Schulz, Axel et al.: "eTourismus: Prozesse und Systeme", 2nd edition, 2015, P. 24
[193] See Conrad, Saskia: "Mobile Applikationen im Tourismus", 2013, P. 13

are usually only created for a particular task area, and customized and optimized for that area.[194]

So the following definition of mobile app may be derived:

> *Mobile app refers to a piece of application software for mobile devices and mobile operating systems.*

Due to the great success of the iPhone launched in 2007 by US company Apple and the publication of the Android smartphone operating system in 2008 by US company Google, the term has increasingly come to refer to applications that can be installed as additional software on mobile devices such as smartphones and tablets to extend the functionality of the device.[195]

3.9.2 Types of mobile app

One may distinguish between three types of mobile app: native apps, web apps and hybrid apps. To assist understanding, we shall now briefly explain these three types:

---

[194] See Schilling, Karolina: "Apps machen", 2016, P. 7
[195] See Wächter, Mark: "Mobile Strategy", 2016, P. 6-7 and Jaser, Michael: "Evaluation, Bewertung und Implementierung verschiedener Cross-Plattform Development Ansätze für Mobile Internet Devices auf Basis von Web-Technologien", 2011, P. 1

- **Native apps**

  Native apps are applications that are customized for the platform concerned, use APIs and libraries to access the hardware, and can be installed onto the devices themselves. They are programmed in the language required by the platform and the app is usually distributed from a central point (e.g. Apple AppStore, Google Play Store).

- **Web apps**

  Web apps are mobile websites that are developed based on web technologies such as HTML, CSS and JavaScript. The term 'web app' is not restricted to mobile websites, however, so in principle every application on the web can be regarded as a web app. Though there is no precise definition, the term is mainly used in relation to HTML5. These are offline-capable websites that are customized for mobile devices and based on native apps. The technical background is the same as with normal websites, but using HTML5 functions achieves better platform integration (e.g. via location-based services and integrating sensors).

  The main down-side is currently the limited access to hardware of software functions on the device platform. For example, the camera on the device cannot be controlled, or the calendar cannot be accessed.[196] Progress is now being made in this direction and one may anticipate that web apps will soon offer many more functionalities than they currently do.

- **Hybrid apps**

  Hybrid apps are a mixture of web app and native app. The aim is to balance out the advantages and disadvantages of the native and web apps.

  Hybrid frameworks are usually based on web technologies and enable cross-platform apps to be developed which the user cannot distinguish from native apps. To simplify, a hybrid framework is a container for a web app.[197]

Development is currently proceeding very rapidly in the web apps area. An ever-increasing number of functions that were previously restricted to native apps are now also available for web apps. It may be assumed that hybrid apps, as a transitional solution, will be superseded by pure web apps in the long term.

---

[196] See Eugster, Jörg et al.: "Die ganze Welt des Online-Marketings", 2015, P. 146
[197] See Böhringer, Joachim et al.: "Kompendium der Mediengestaltung", 6th, fully revised and extended edition, 2015, P. 623

3.9.3 Using mobile apps in hotels

The variety of potential uses for mobile apps in hotels ranges from simply displaying information about the hotel (text and photos) through to the guest managing their entire hotel stay (check-in to check-out).[198]

We shall now describe the main options for using mobile apps in hotels. As has already been mentioned, most digital guest experience tools require the guest to install a mobile app. So it is inevitable that there will be overlaps between potential applications described in previous sections and the list that follows. However, the list makes no claim to be complete.

- **Check-in**

    Check-in using an app can work in different ways. Prior to their arrival day, the guest is sent a notification about using the app to check in. Then, when the guest arrives, the front-desk employee has all the data in front of them and the check-in process is shortened. It is also possible that the guest is recognized when they set foot in the lobby, using the app and beacons, the guest checks themselves in, and can then use the app to also open the hotel room door.

---

[198] See Xiang, Zheng / Thssyadiah, Iis (Hrsg.): "Information and Communication Technologies in Tourism 2014", 2014, P. 47ff.

- **Indoor navigation**

An integrated indoor navigation system can give the hotel guest added value. After checking in, the app can guide the guest to their room. Guests can quickly become disoriented in large hotels in particular. If a hotel has more than one restaurant, for example, the app can navigate the guest to the right restaurant.

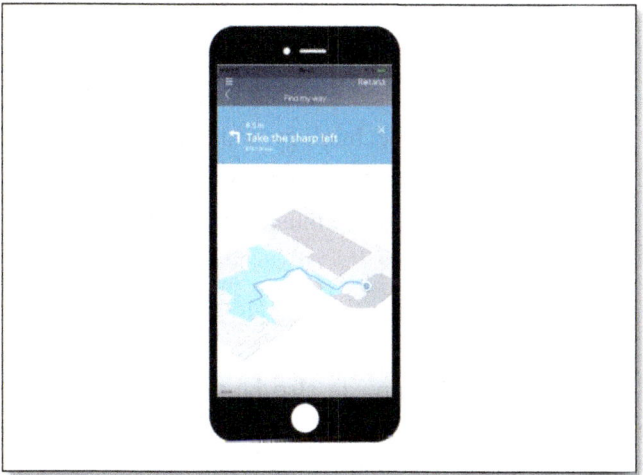

Fig. 17: "Example of an app with indoor navigation"
Source: Neorcha, 2016

In an emergency situation (evacuation) the hotel app can help the guest leave the hotel via the shortest route using the navigation function.

157

- **Hotel information**

  The most common application scenario for hotel apps is distributing information about the hotel. When does the restaurant or swimming pool open? Is there a spa area or ironing room? When does the room need to be vacated? Ultimately, all the information found in traditional guest folders can also be shown in the app.

- **Room controls**

  Given appropriate interfaces, a mobile app can be used to control all the technology within the hotel room. The lights in the room can be switched on and off, the climate control system adjusted and music streamed.

- **Room service**

  The hotel's app can also be used to order room services. This could mean missing toiletries such as lavatory paper or towels, as well as food and drink. Tables can also be reserved in the hotel restaurant, or a spa treatment can be booked.

- **Concierge service**

  All the services a concierge can provide could also be installed in a hotel app – from organizing theater tickets to calling a taxi. Wake-up calls are probably not required as a smartphone has its own alarm function.

- **Reviews and feedback**

An important function that a hotel app can include is the opportunity to give feedback and reviews. [199] With this function, the hotel gets the capability to respond directly to the guest's complaints. Unlike when reviews are submitted on portals such as TripAdvisor and HolidayCheck, a solution can be found during the guest's stay so that a potentially negative rating at a later stage is avoided, or even converted into a positive one.

- **Payment**

The guest should also be given the opportunity to settle their bill with the hotel app, whether this is done using payment services such as PayPal, Google Wallet, Apple Pay, Bitcoins or a credit card account saved in the app. [200]

It should also be possible to use the hotel app to pay using loyalty points.

---

[199] See Stauss, Bernd / Seidel, Wolfgang: "Beschwerdemanagement: Unzufriedene Kunden als profitable Zielgruppe", 5th, fully revised edition, 2014, P. 110f.

[200] To ensure PCI-compatibility and save the credit card data securely, the tokenization process is applied. With this, credit card numbers in the intended systems are replaced by a random value (token) and then saved.

Fig. 18: "Option to pay using Apple Pay"
Source: Iris, 2016

- **Tour guide**

  The hotel app can act as a virtual tour guide, taking guests around the city to see the sights and hip places or around a local museum.[201] This would positively translate the guest experience in the hotel to the environment outside the hotel, improving guest satisfaction.

- **Transport**

  The concierge app used by Hilton's Conrad Hotels, for example, enables the guest to arrange transport from and to

---

[201] See Ray, Nilanjan; "Emerging Innovative Marketing Strategies in the Tourism Industry", 2015, P. 87

the airport or railway station.[202] The hotel app can also integrate the ability to call a taxi.[203] A partnership with Uber might be feasible in this context, if the guest does not have their own Uber account. The Uber bill could then be settled via the hotel bill.

- **Hotel room bookings**

Though the guest is already in the hotel, there ought to be a capability to make a future booking for a hotel room. A discount voucher could be used as an incentive if the guest opts for a future visit during their current stay.

- **Loyalty program**

The guest must be able to configure personalized settings for the loyalty program in the hotel app. An overview of the points earned to date and the ability to use those points in the hotel have a positive effect on the digital guest experience. An app user should also be able to register for the loyalty program if they are not already a member. As an

---

[202] See Weissmann, Saya: "5 Hotel Brands With Useful Mobile Apps", 2013, http://digiday.com/brands/5-hotel-brands-with-useful-mobile-apps/

[203] See Mahnicke, Rüdiger: "Business Travel Management: Praxis-Know-How für den Einkäufer", 2013, P. 31

incentive for registering, the user would be given their first points.[204]

3.9.4 Challenges for mobile apps

The main challenge in using mobile apps lies in downloading and installing the hotel app on the guest's smartphone. Many smartphone users have become cautious about installing apps, as they already have many apps installed and only focus on using a small number of them. [205] Hotels are now often using the "WhatsApp" application to communicate with guests. Chatbots can also be useful in this context.

So any additional app needs to offer the guest distinct added value. So in the app store there needs to be a very easily understandable description and a clear explanation of the added value. The app's design is crucial to its success. Users need to understand why the app is being installed, what data will be used and how the application will communicate with them.[206]

For example, a simple app design showing some hotel basics could be counter-productive and impact negatively on the hotel's image.

---

[204] See anon.: "5 Tips for Designing a Hotel Loyalty Program that really works", 2015, http://www.webrezpro.com/5-tips-for-designing-a-hotel-loyalty-program-that-really-works/

[205] See anon.: "App Store Trends: Users Spend More Time in Less Apps", 2016, http://adtechdaily.com/2016/11/15/app-store-trends-users-spend-time-less-apps/

[206] See Böpple, Oliver / Glende, Sebastian / Schauber, Cornelia: "Innovative Einkaufserlebnisse mit Beacon-Technologie gestalten" in: Linnhoff-Popien, Claudia / Zaddach, Michael / Grahl, Andreas: "Marktplätze im Umbruch – Digitale Strategien für Services im Mobilen Internet", 2015, P. 303

It would also create a psychological barrier to using other digital guest experience tools. The big challenge in designing the application lies in integrating the necessary functions in the best possible, balanced way.

Not every service available via the app needs to be delivered by the hotel. For transport, an integrated existing taxi app such as MyTaxi or Uber could be used, or GetYourGuide could be integrated for tour guide purposes. The challenge is to integrate these 3rd party providers. Potential integration requirements need to be considered when creating the application.

With these potential applications, the interface is often a challenge. Controlling the technology in the room and ordering room service require different interface customizations. Mobile check-in requires an interface to the PMS, and the loyalty program needs a CRM interface.

Finally, there are significant challenges in terms of keeping the app current and upgrading platforms. This means that platform evaluations may influence the application's functionalities and that the application will need to be adjusted. In customizing the interfaces, there are knock-on costs involved in changing the applications.

3.9.5 Return on investment on mobile apps

There is little sense in a hotel offering its own app merely to have its own app. Without a dedicated strategy and clear objectives, the financial and human resources required are better saved and invested in the hotel website instead, to optimize it for mobile. [207]

The return on investing in an application comes particularly from increasing guest satisfaction and improving guest loyalty. While using mobile apps has direct financial effects, guest loyalty, in particular, generates increased revenue in the long term.

- **Increased revenue**

  An app alone will not increase revenue. The guest has to actively engage with the application's offerings. So it is a good idea to send push messages with special offers (discount vouchers) to the guest's smartphone during their stay, in order to then conduct a transaction (table reservation, spa appointment, etc.) using the app. Another option is to send the guest a pre-stay mail telling them which functions the hotel app will offer during their stay and that they can redeem their existing points. In this way, new guests can, at the same time, be made aware of the application.

  Otherwise the causal connection between use of the app and increased revenue will be difficult to measure due to other influences.

---

[207] See Kamps, Ingo: "Einstieg in erfolgreiches Mobile Marketing", 2015, P. 10

■ **Guest loyalty**

If the app gives the guest real added value it can considerably boost guest loyalty. The guest has all their relevant data (personal details, preferences, stays), and the points they have earned, in the app. So the app becomes the main port-of-call for the guest in terms of their loyalty membership. If the app is capable of giving the guest bespoke, personalized offers, it has great potential to positively influence the guest's loyalty, and therefore to help optimize revenue per guest over the long term.

■ **Guest satisfaction**

As stated previously in relation to other guest experience tools, optimizing the check-in process increases guest satisfaction. All the relevant, necessary guest information can be stored in an app and be accessed by the receptionist to speed up check-in. Check-in could also be automated, dispensing with any contact with the hotel's staff, which would particularly increase satisfaction amongst so-called silent travelers and the millennials target group.[208]

Shortening check-in times is not the only way in which guest satisfaction can be increased using the hotel's app. All the ideas that have been described to simplify the

---

[208] See anon.: "Shhh…There's A New Silent Traveler In Town (And Here's Why They're Important)", 2014, http://blog.leonardo.com/shhhtheres-a-new-silent-traveler-in-town-and-heres-why-theyre-important/

guest's stay have a positive effect on the guest's satisfaction and digital experience.

To conclude, it should be pointed out that the app can only succeed if used in conjunction with all the other digital guest experience tools and all of the hotel's other systems. Only if the guest experience management system is well-aligned can the app become the guest's main port-of-call and the digital guest experience tools become successful.

Chapter 4

Barriers to implementation

4 Barriers to implementation

Chapter 3 described the various digital guest experience tools in detail, and Chapter 2 looked at why hotels ought to invest in these tools in the future. Deploying digital guest experience tools is not simple, however, as there are barriers to their implementation. We shall now examine these barriers.

4.1 Strategic barriers

In the hotel sector, guest experience management is part of corporate strategy. Digital guest experience tools are used to implement this strategy operationally, in the digital area. However, the strategic definition often fails to specify what the deployment of innovative digital technologies in the hotel business is intended to achieve. At times there is no clear, overall, digital strategic aim. So the successful deployment of digital guest experience tools in the hotel business is largely dictated by the digital strategic objective and the organizational implementation.

Frequently, however, a poor, or poorly-informed, understanding within senior management levels is a major barrier for innovative technologies. Amongst many medium-sized hotel groups, digitalization is still of minor importance to the corporate strategy. Ultimately, this is also reflected in the budget allocation.[209] While it is true that management recognize the need to invest in digital

---

[209] See Glattes, Karin: "Der Konkurrenz ein Kundenerlebnis voraus: Customer Experience Management", 2016, P. XI

distribution and the hotel's website, there is little understanding of the basic requirements. The need for the hotel to have its own CRM system, problems relating to interfaces and the associated investment are underestimated. Valuable data that can be combined with data acquired externally is collected at every digital touchpoint. However, technological tools such as interfaces and a CRM program are required if this data is to be used effectively and help grow the business.

Alongside the big challenge of data usage ('big data'), the next technological innovation with wide-ranging implications for the hotel sector, conversational commerce, is around the corner. Many hotel groups, essentially, require a digital transformation with a deep understanding of the digital interlinking of all the company's areas if they are to be able to face the digital challenges of the future.[210]

With digitalization spreading through hotel businesses, and with digital transformation, power struggles and role conflicts occur amongst senior levels. The hotel operation, previously the domain of the Chief Operating Officer, is now being influenced by the digital area, which might come under a different executive mandate. One solution, here, might be to appoint a Chief Digital Officer whose influence will cut across every area, as in a matrix organization.

---

[210] See IBM Institute for Business Value: "Digital Transformation Creating New Business Models Where Digital Meets Physical", 2011, P. 2

Only if the strategic prerequisites for the digital guest experience tools are in place, and if a holistic system is set up to manage the tools, will the digital guest experience tools be successful and make a valuable contribution within the company in terms of the hotel operation.[211] This includes increasing revenue, improving guest satisfaction and loyalty, and innovative image as a differentiating feature. The future of the hotel industry is not merely digital, but also different, so it is essential that business models differ from those in place prior to the digital age.[212]

4.2 Organizational barriers

On the organizational side, it should be borne in mind that, despite the potential savings in the personnel area, appropriate resources and expertise are required to, first, implement the digital guest experience tools and then use them. Competent employees need to be given the task of planning the areas in which the digital guest experience tools will be used, and they need to be given the necessary time, and be capable of understanding the complex technical relationships. It is advisable that, first of all, the hotel's digital reality is sketched, the current value creation chains, and the actors involved, are analyzed, and guests' requirements are recorded.[213] Based on this, the objectives are defined which are to

---

[211] Drawing on Smith, Shaun / Wheeler, Joe: "Managing the Customer Experience: Turning Customers into Advocates", 2002, P. 2
[212] See Hoffmeister, Christian: "Digitale Geschäftsmodelle richtig einschätzen", 2013, P. 2
[213] See Schallmo, Daniel: "Jetzt digital transformieren: So gelingt die erfolgreiche Digitale Transformation Ihres Geschäftsmodells", 2016, P. 21

be achieved by deploying the digital guest experience tools. During the implementation, the guests' specific digital experiences are pinned down, as is the digital value creation network with the partners involved. The resources and capabilities required for the implementation are also noted.

Another important area of expertise is data analysis. The larger the data volume, the more difficult the analyses ('big data'). The challenge lies in deriving the relevant conclusions and using them to successfully address guests.[214] Coping with these volumes of data, and making best use of them, offers many benefits, as previous sections have described. Guests need to be addressed in a way that is consistent and in tune with the various touchpoints and their different preferences.

A large amount of data needs to be summarized in the operational interaction profiles. By segmenting and analyzing the interaction paths from the guest's perspective, the customer journey insights become clearer. Priorities for analysis need to be set early on, based on the different interaction paths that depend on the event and the person. Customers' needs and interaction patterns are used, here, as the basis for the segmentation.

---

[214] See Schmidt, Holger: "Michael E. Porter: Das Internet der Dinge verändert Unternehmen stärker als alle bisherigen IT-Entwicklungen", 2015, https://netzoekonom.de/2015/05/25/michael-e-porter-das-internet-der-dinge-veraendert-unternehmen-staerker-als-alle-bisherigen-it-entwicklungen/

All the potential of the digital guest experience tools can only be unlocked by analyzing the data collected and using it for the purposes of bespoke personalization. Producing reports for the hotel's, or hotel group's, senior managers can also be an organizational bottleneck and a barrier in terms of measuring success.

Organizational process structures are another organizational barrier. Changing a process is always initially a barrier, as the new process needs to be understood and, ultimately, complied with, by staff and also by the guests.

4.3 Technological barriers

The main technological barrier is the problem of interfaces. Digital guest experience tools need to be integrated into existing systems. However, heterogeneous systems in the hotel industry which can only communicate with each other to a limited degree, mean that the same data cannot be accessed via every channel and that there are often no open interfaces. So introducing digital guest experience tools usually involves a time-consuming migration task.

When implementing tools, there is a need to ensure that the providers have the relevant, licensed interfaces so that the systems can share data with one another. Not having these can lead to expensive customizations and to the deployment of the digital guest experience tools being substantially delayed, which will impede a rapid return on investment. As digital tools to optimize the guest experience become more widespread, the sector ought to come to an agreement on standards relating to interfaces and data sharing.[215]

As mentioned in the various sections on digital guest experience tools, a content management system (CMS) is required that is easy to use and can interact with other systems. The challenge, here, is that all CMSs only work homogeneously, for one digital guest experience tool and do not interact with each other. This means that any integrated, holistic marketing communication is impossible and that hotel staff have extra work to do which, again, creates a psychological barrier.

Many of the tools described need a properly functioning WLAN (WiFi). This requirement is already often a barrier to implementation, since many hotel WLAN systems are out-of-date.

At the latest when implementing digital guest experience tools requires building work and investment in technological infrastructure, a substantial barrier and challenge is involved. So it is advisable to include potential digital guest experience tools in the planning phase, and budget for them, when carrying out room renovations or building work in the hotel.

As the digital guest experience tools can only be effective when using personal guest data, the IT security requirements are considerable. Any rudimentary security in terms of data sharing

---

[215] Waldmax, Max: "Why 2016 needs to be the year of the digital guest standard", 2016, https://www.tnooz.com/article/hotel-guest-experience-digital-standard/

(personal data and details relating to payments) is a major barrier and should be avoided. Particularly in view of the increasing number of hacker attacks, there has to be investment in data security.

The greatest technological barrier, though, is the fact that many hotels and hotel groups do not have a CRM system. Guests' personal data is usually only stored in the PMS and is not used for optimizing revenue or the way guests are addressed.

But an effective CRM system is central to successfully deploying digital guest experience tools. There has to be, and there will be, a change of paradigm in the hotel industry with regard to guests' profile data. It will no longer be the PMS or CRS which are the main systems for guest data, but rather the CRM or in-house profile data systems. Every action taken and every marketing measure (whether digital or traditional) will be based on the guest's profile.

It is also the CRM's role to systematically record any relevant information about guests, and to provide information about profitability, preferences and loyalty. Based on these findings, and enriched with external market data, specific offerings are then developed and delivered effectively, and automatically, via the digital guest experience tools. In the future, only if there is plenty of valid data will it be possible to reap the benefits from predictive analytics, and will it be possible to create undreamed of ways to increase revenue in the hotel using digital guest experience tools.[216]

In the future, for a hotel to be successful, it will have to systematically compile and analyze all guest information, give the central (digital) touchpoints operational support and synchronize them, and manage and integrate all the (digital) communication channels to the guest.[217]

4.4 Financial barriers

Financial barriers continue to be the main obstacle to implementing innovative technologies.[218] This barrier can only be overcome, and managers made to understand the need to invest in future business models, through a plausible business case. Even though some technologies, such as digital payments, are a hygiene factor, clear business plans with a defined return on investment can be drawn up for other tools.

This book aims to provide some support in this context, as it has shown the areas where return on investment can be achieved.

At this point, the technological barriers again need to be mentioned. Technical implementation often involves spending that could have

---

[216] Predictive analytics is an area of data mining that deals with predicting the probable future and trends.
[217] See Hippner, Hajo / Wilde Klaus-Dieter: "Grundlagen des CRM: Konzepte und Gestaltung", 2006, P. 13ff.
[218] See anon. "Adobe Digital Roadblock Report 2016", 2016, P. 28

been avoided with good planning and a detailed analysis of requirements during the design phase.

4.5 Psychological barriers

Up until now, little consideration has been given to questions concerning the acceptance of the products and potential barriers to use. A key factor in people's willingness to use them is the uncertainty about potential risks, a lack of understanding of their pros and cons, and people's limited experience of using these types of technology.[219] But the type of technology, the context of use and personal factors such as age, technology generation and gender are significant to the tolerance of risk and uncertainty.[220]

As stated in section 3.2.4, in social terms Germany tends to be a land of technology skeptics. So it is advisable to involve potential users when developing digital guest experience applications. This involvement includes any worries the users may have, and can help improve acceptance.

Another must, when deploying digital guest experience tools, is "easy to use": guests should find the digital guest experience tools uncomplicated to use and simple to understand. [221] Frustration

---

[219] See Qattawi, Lisa: "Barrieren im Wissensmanagement", 2006, P. 65ff.
[220] See Ziefle, Martina: "Ungewissheit und Unsicherheit bei der Einführung neuer Technologien", o.A., P. 83
[221] See Watkinson, Matt: "The Ten Principles Behind Great Customer Experience", 2013, P. 23

should be avoided so that success is not put at risk and harmed for the long term. When introducing the digital guest experience tools to the guest it is also helpful to use incentive systems (for example, discount vouchers or other perks) to get them to engage with the technology.

The hotel's staff, too, need to be persuaded to accept the, mostly highly innovative, guest experience tools. In this context, the technical tools need to work correctly. The corporate strategy also needs to include the relevant digital aims, and staff have to be told about the tools' added value so that they can acquire an understanding of the need and the benefits. Senior company management have to clearly communicate the areas in which the tools will be used and the changes in the areas of working conditions, in order to allay fears about job losses. Training and development also help to motivate staff to deal with, and better understand, digital experience tools.[222] The change induced by digitalization is not just technological change – it also needs to be reflected in cultural change within the company, and to engage the staff.[223]

If the employees' psychological barriers prove too stubborn, digitalization will not succeed in the hotel operation.

---

[222] See Sauter, Werner / Scholz, Christina: "Kompetenzorientiertes Wissensmanagement: Gesteigerte Performance mit dem Erfahrungswissen aller Mitarbeiter", 2015, P. 30

[223] See Voigt, Kai-Ingo: "Kulturbewußtes Management – Wandel von Unternehmensstrategie und Unternehmenskultur", in: Hansmann, Karl-Werner (ed.): "Management des Wandels", 2012, P. 55

4.6 Legal barriers

Internationally operating hotel companies must comply with local laws. In Germany, for example, there are many legal barriers. The main one is data protection. In the provisions of the BDSG (Data Protection Act) and the TMG (Telemedia Act), German data protection law states that merely processing personal data requires prior consent from those concerned. This consent may be a considerable barrier to use for some of the digital guest experience tools that have been described. With automatic face recognition, in particular, getting the guest's permission beforehand is counterproductive. The benefit derives from the hotel employee having access to all the guest information required without asking them for it.

Even if the right to privacy is a highly developed area of law in Germany and Europe it may be assumed that data protection law will change over the course of the coming years. Younger generations will probably have technology requirements that might cause those responsible for data protection to alter data protection legislation.

As regards hotel staff, there are also legal challenges that need to be taken into account when introducing digital guest experience tools. The German Co-Determination Act states that employees'

179

representatives have to be notified before any technical installations are introduced which could impact on the employees' work.[224]

It is advisable that legal requirements are studied carefully, and taken into account, when implementing digital guest experience tools in order not to endanger a successful deployment. Should there be any doubts, input should be obtained from external lawyers with the relevant expertise.

4.7 Barriers: summary

To conclude, it should be pointed out that all these barriers are interlinked. so they need to be avoided or eliminated if the integrating of digital guest experience tools is to be a success.

---

[224] See Art. 87 Para. 1 Clause. 6 BetrVG (German Works Constitution Act) and Art. 106 ff. BetrVG

Chapter 5

Conclusion and the future

5 Conclusion and the future

The digitalization of entire business models is not just a challenge in the hotel industry, but one facing all sectors over the coming years. But there are opportunities in the hotel sector, particularly in the hotel stay area, which were previously undreamed of. The digital transformation of existing touchpoints and technological innovations are generating completely new opportunities for hotels to remain in constant contact with their guests, and to give the guests suitable information and offerings at the right time, with no wastage.

Tools like digital room assignment and mobile check-in are simplifying processes and thereby creating benefits for guests and staff. Intelligent hotel rooms are bringing guests tangible gains in terms of convenience – the guest opening the hotel door with their own device, and controlling the technology in the room with a concierge tablet or the app on their smartphone. Digital innovations such as digital signage are not only creating the capability for guests to navigate around the hotel effectively, but are also being used to generate new sources of income. Guests and hoteliers alike can benefit from the use of beacons.

However, for these digital guest experience tools to be used effectively, the systems in the hotel need to be networked and a very good customer relationship management (CRM) system is essential. Only by networking the systems in the hotel and integrating the digital guest experience tools, while taking the stored guest profiles and information into account, will the ability

183

be created to address guests in an effective way to improve guest satisfaction and revenue and reduce costs.

To summarize, the use of digital guest experience tools offers benefits in the following areas in particular:

- **Competitive advantage:** The hotel's core service – the overnight stay – can easily be replaced. So hotels need to create profiles using additional services and make use of the competitive advantages that currently exist by using digital guest experience tools.

- **Process optimization:** New technologies can help the hotel to respond more swiftly to guests' questions and requests. Moreover, process steps in the hotel are simplified and process complexity is reduced by a largely digitalized process chain.

- **Increased effectiveness:** Reducing process complexity also impacts positively on the hotel operation's overall effectiveness. All the guest-related measures can be deployed more effectively and more guests can be served with greater quality. Guest can be looked after in a more differentiated way, and strategically relevant guests (VIPs) can be given closer attention.

- **Guest satisfaction:** The outcomes of optimizing processes lead to improvements in how guests are looked after and the personal attention they are given. This has a positive impact on guest satisfaction.

- **Cost reductions:** Digitalization enables small and medium-sized hotel operations to make significant cost reductions. Processes can be shortened or eliminated entirely. Personnel costs can be cut or existing staff can be deployed optimally.

- **Increased revenues:** Using digital guest experience tools can increase revenues in many areas of the hotel operation.

- **Image optimization:** Last but not least, deploying digital guest experience tools enables hotels to position their own services and their own brand as innovative. This positioning can have a positive effect on the hotel's image, differentiating it from the competition, providing there is a unique selling point.

To summarize, though, it also needs to be pointed out that by linking the various digital guest experience tools it is difficult to directly measure and clearly assign the positive effects on revenues and satisfaction. Success can only be judged by taking a holistic view.

185

The future

This book makes it clear that research into the digital guest experience and using tools in the hotel industry is still at a very early stage. Future academic research is needed to analyze the effect of different types of guest experience on the company's success and to establish the digital guest centricity approach in the industry.

Up-and-coming technologies need to be identified and examined with respect to their potential deployment in the hotel.

Even though the robot technologies described in this book may still be odd to many guests, this innovation will become increasingly common in the coming years and the image of robots will change to the extent that distinguishing them from human beings will be a challenge.

For the coming generations, the personalized approach involved in digital signage, beacons, apps and other digital experience tools will be accepted as a matter of course. This target group will punish hotels that operate standardized communications. The new generation of hotel guests will understand the algorithms behind the technologies and be able to judge them. There will be rising expectations of digital guest experience tools.

Hotels' in-room technology is also only beginning to undergo a digital revolution. Guests will expect the hotel room to be as technologically well-equipped as their own home. The ability to log into their own Netflix account on an LED TV will be expected, as

186

will a WiFi that operates faultlessly. Radio in the bath will be regarded as self-evident but, in contrast, a mirror that has an integrated television and connects via Bluetooth to the guest's smartphone to read mails while the guest gets ready in the morning will, in the future, be hoped for and, without any doubt, increasingly expected.

In the future, electric cars will become increasingly common, and the hotel sector can come to play a key role in providing access to infrastructure in the form of charging stations, contributing to e-mobility in society. During their stay, guests' vehicles can be charged in the basement garage.

Other innovations, such as nanotechnologies, have been omitted completely from this book. However, their influence on the guest experience and guest engagement will be considerable. Networks of sensors based on "smartdust" can be installed in hotels to continually monitor the environment and adjust the hotel to suit guests' needs. Nanotechnologies can be deployed to change the color of entire walls in the hotel lobby, or huge projection spaces can create the sensation of one being, for example, in the middle of a primeval forest.

Emerging neurotechnologies can also add to the guest experience. In the future, guests will be able to choose a dream from a virtual catalog and enjoy it while sleeping.

Improvements in hologram technology can make staying in the hotel room a real experience, taking virtual reality to the next level.

Not only by being able to transform the entire room into a fantasy world, but also by being able to place a hologram of a personal fitness trainer in the room or maybe by virtually transporting the guest's family into the room from their distant home to enjoy an evening meal.

While it is true that 3D printing is still in its infancy, it could revolutionize room service in the near future. The meal the guest wants could actually be printed out in their room, for instance. The hotel guest could also use a 3D printer to get a toothbrush or comb they may have forgotten.

In the future, hotel stays will be paid for using biometric methods such as face recognition, the guest's heartbeat or a fingerprint. Blockchain technology will be used to make payment processes more secure. Blockchain technology will also improve the hotel's loyalty program for the guest and optimize processes in the hotel.

Taking findings relating to the human This allocation would be blocked out for rooms that bring in more revenue which would no longer be available for sale limbic system and technological innovations, interdisciplinary teams of interior architects, interior designers, communications experts and digital specialists will develop new types of design (lead experience concepts) that enable an all-encompassing customer experience for the hotel sector. Interior designers will also ensure that hotels are designed with a view to encouraging guests to take photos and share them on social media networks.

In the future, the entire hotel stay will be a digital experience, and guests will no longer be loyal to brands, but to experiences!

About the author

Björn Radde currently works at Sabre Hospitality Solutions as Director Digital Experience in the EMEA region. Sabre acquired Trust International where Björn owned the role of the Vice President Digital Marketing within the product management unit and worldwide responsible for all digital marketing products and services of the company. Previously, Björn was Director Digital Marketing & E-Commerce at Okanda, an internet startup in the meetings business, and Head of E-Commerce at the Steigenberger Hotel Group.

At Okanda Bjoern was member of the management board and also responsible for product development. In his strategic position at Steigenberger he had shaped the electronic distribution landscape of the hotel group. During his time at Steigenberger Björn Radde was also a member of the customer advisory Board of Trust International and was able to incorporate his expertise into product development projects. The pilot for augmented reality was one of Björn's last projects at Steigenberger.

After studying economics with a focus on online marketing and e-commerce, he initially worked at T-Online International and later at Deutsche Telekom within the Products & Innovation business

190

unit, where he focused on personalization, targeting and digital customer touchpoint management.

Björn Radde regularly publishes articles in the field of digital marketing and innovations, is an interviewee for the trade press and he is also speaker at various hospitality industry events.

Bibliography

A

Allen, Aaron: "Restaurant Marketing Ideas: 10 Examples of Augmented Reality", 2016, http://aaronallen.com/blog/restaurant-marketing/augmented-reality

Ambwani, Meenakshi Verma: "From 'Whitney Rack' to electronic reservation systems", 2013, http://www.thehindubusinessline.com/economy/hospitalit y-sector-from-whitney-rack-to-electronic-reservation-systems/article5064873.ece

Andrews, Sudhier: "Hotel Front Office – A Training Manual", 3rd Edition, 2013

anon.: "2016 Asia Pacific hotel performance", 2017, http://www.hospitalitynet.org/news/4080566.html

anon.: "Mexican tourism industry experiencing its best performance ever", 2017, http://www.tourism-review.com/mexican-tourism-sector-booming-news5324

anon.: "Was sich Gäste im Hotel am meisten wünschen", 2012, https://www.welt.de/reise/article106131007/Was-sich-Gaeste-im-Hotel-am-meisten-wuenschen.html

anon.: "NH Hotel Group verzeichnet starkes Wachstum", 2016, http://www.tophotel.de/20-news/7916-gesch%C3%A4ftszahlen-nh-hotel-group-verzeichnet-starkes-wachstum.html

anon.: DEHOGA economic survey autumn 2016

anon.: German Federal Statistical Office: "Binnenhandel, Gastgewerbe, Tourismus - Ergebnisse der Monatserhebung im Tourismus", Subject-matter series 6 Series 7.1, 2016

anon.: "Wettbewerbsvorteile durch Robotics realisieren" in: "Detecon Management Report", Issue 2, 2016

anon.: "Service-Roboter: Kühle Drinks vom elektronischen Barkeeper", 2012, http://www.handelsblatt.com/technik/forschung-innovation/service-roboter-noch-fehlt-die-akzeptanz-fuer-dic-service-maschinen/7259486-2.html

anon.: "Interactive Digital Signage helps guests find their way" in: „Lodging" No. 34, 2008

anon.: "The Hotel Customer Journey", 2015, https://www.hotelgenius.co/index.php/the-hotel-customer-journey/

anon.: "Restaurants der Zukunft: Persönlicher Service weiterhin sehr wichtig" in: "Gastronomie und Hotellerie", 2016, http://www.gastronomie-hotellerie.com/restaurants-der-zukunft-persoenlicher-service-weiterhin-sehr-wichtig

anon.: "Augmented reality start-up aims for cleaner rooms", 2017, http://ehotelier.com/global/2017/03/22/augmented-reality-startup-aims-cleaner-rooms/

anon.: Signbox Microsystems: "Digital Signage Facial Recognition with signEye", 2016, https://signbox.tv/digital-signage-products/digital-signage-facial-recognition

anon.: Samsung whitepaper: "Zeichen der Zeit – Digital Signage als Werbe- und Informationsmedium der Zukunft", 2013

anon.: "Die strategische Bedeutung von RevPar und Bewertungen", 2015, http://www.customer-alliance.com/de/strategie-revpar-bewertungen/

anon.: "5 Tips for Designing a Hotel Loyalty Program that really works", 2015, http://www.webrezpro.com/5-tips-for-designing-a-hotel-loyalty-program-that-really-works/

anon.: "App Store Trends: Users Spend More Time in Less Apps", 2016, http://adtechdaily.com/2016/11/15/app-store-trends-users-spend-time-less-apps/

anon.: "Shhh…There's A New Silent Traveler In Town (And Here's Why They're Important)", 2014, http://blog.leonardo.com/shhhtheres-a-new-silent-traveler-in-town-and-heres-why-theyre-important/

anon.: "Adobe Digital Roadblock Report 2016", 2016

anon.: "Rift, Vive, Hololense – Wie VR-Brillen 2016 das Smart Home erobern", 2016, https://www.smart-wohnen.de/virtual-reality/artikel/rift-vive-hololense-wie-vr-brillen-2016-das-smart-home-erobern/

anon.: "Hotels bieten eigene VR-Brillen für Pornografie an", 2016, http://www.gulli.com/news/27379-hotels-bieten-eigene-vr-brillen-fuer-pornografie-an-2016-04-21

anon.: "Marriott Hotels Introduces The First Ever In-Room Virtual Reality Travel Experience", 2015, http://news.marriott.com/2015/09/marriott-hotels-introduces-the-first-ever-in-room-virtual-reality-travel-experience/

anon.: "Zielsicher – Beacons im Hotel", 2015, https://www.onm.de/agentur/news/artikel/zielsicher-beacons-im-hotel/

anon.: "App Store Trends: Users Spend More Time in Less Apps", 2016, http://adtechdaily.com/2016/11/15/app-store-trends-users-spend-time-less-apps/

anon.: "Password to Marketers Meeting: Digital" in: "The World Street Journal", 2007

anon.: "Suitepads dürfen Telefone im Hotelzimmer ersetzen", 2015, http://www.gastronomie-hotellerie.com/suitepads-duerfen-telefone-im-hotelzimmer-ersetzen

anon.: "Was hat Meckerpotenial? Die Top10 der häufigsten Beschwerden in Hotels", 2010, http://www.trustyou.com/reisebranche/was-hat-meckerpotential-die-top10-der-haufigsten-beschwerden-in-hotels?lang=de

Auel, Kersten: "Personal Indoor Assistant: Den richtigen Weg finden mit Augmented Reality", 2015, https://www.heise.de/ix/meldung/Personal-Indoor-Assistant-Den-richtigen-Weg-finden-mit-Augmented-Reality-2655997.html

Azuma, Ronald: "A Survey of Augmented Reality" in: "Presence: Teleoperators and Virtual Enviroments" 1997, P. 355-385

Azuma, Ronald: "Overview of Augmented Reality" in: Siggraph: "Proceedings of the Conference on Siggraph 2004 course notes", 2004

B

Bagemihl, Jens: "Die strategische Bedeutung von Yield Management im Hotelgewerbe", 1994

Balakrishnan, Anita: "Wynn Las Vegas to add Amazon Alexa to all hotel rooms", 2016, http://www.cnbc.com/2016/12/14/wynn-las-vegas-to-add-amazon-alexa-to-all-hotel-rooms.html

Bente, Gary et al.: "Virtuelle Realität als Gegenstand und Methode in der Psychologie" in: Bente, Gary et al. (ed.): "Virtuelle Realitäten", 2002

Bente, Gary et al. (ed.): "Virtuelle Realitäten", 2002

Bhakta, Vikas: "5 Tips for Attracting the Silent Traveler", 2015, https://www.bookstaygo.com/blog-for-hotels/5-tips-hotels-for-attracting-the-silent-traveler

Binckenbanck, Lars / Elste, Rainer (ed.): "Digitalisierung im Vertrieb – Strategien zum Einsatz neuer Technologien in Vertriebsorganisationen", 2016

Blischke, Johannes: "Betriebssysteme für Smartphones", 2015

Böpple, Oliver / Glende, Sebastian / Schauber, Cornelia: "Innovative Einkaufserlebnisse mit Beacon-Technologie

gestalten" in: Linnhoff-Popien, Claudia / Zaddach,
Michael / Grahl, Andreas: "Markpläzte im Umbruch –
Digitale Strategien für Services im Mobilen Internet",
2015

Böhringer, Joachim et al.: "Kompendium der
Mediengestaltung", 6th Edition, 2015

Bordel, Stefan: "Microsoft rüstet Bing-Suche mit Augmented
Reality auf", 2016,
http://www.internetworld.de/onlinemarketing/microsoft/m
icrosoft-ruestet-bing-suche-augmented-reality-
1152870.html

Borison, Rebecca: "Marriott Hotels reimagines travel with
augmented reality", 2013,
http://www.mobilemarketer.com/cms/news/software-
technology/16391.html

Braun, Alexander: "Chatbots in der Kundenkommunikation",
2003

Breiter, Andreas / Fischer, Arne: "Implementierung von IT
Service-Management", 2011

Brendel, Nadine: "(Mobile) Augmented Reality – Hype oder
nachhaltiges Marketinginstrument?", 2011,
http://www.marketing-

boerse.de/Fachartikel/details/Mobile-Augmented-Reality-
%96-Hype-oder-nachhaltiges-Marketinginstrument/33276

Bruhn, Manfred / Hadwich, Karsten (ed.): "Customer
Experience: Forum Dienstleistungsmanagement", 2012

Bruns, Matthias: "Virtual Reality – Eine Analyse der
Schlüsseltechnologie aus der Perspektive des strategischen
Managements", 2015

Brusilovski, Peter / Kommers, Piet: "Multimedia, Hypermedia
and Virtual Reality", 1994

Burmann, Christoph / König, Verena / Meurer, Jörg (ed.):
"Identitätsbasierte Luxusmarkenführung", 2012

C

Callahan, Sean: "Hotels can usher in the future of hospitality by
deploying innovative beacon technology", 2015,
http://www.digitalsocialretail.com/hotels-can-usher-in-
the-future-of-hospitality-by-deploying-innovative-beacon-
technology/

Callahan, Sean: "Gyms and Fitness Centers work out better with
wireless Beacons", 2016,

http://www.digitalsocialretail.com/gyms-and-fitness-
centers-work-out-better-with-wireless-beacons/

Castanon, Raul: "Conversational technologies will be a key
game changer in 2017", 2016,
https://chatbotslife.com/conversational-technologies-will-
be-a-key-game-changer-in-2017-
18ca0555553c#.l62dpx7dq

Chang, Christina: "Augmented Reality Applications in the
Tourism Industry", 2016,
http://www.augment.com/blog/augmented-reality-in-
tourism/

Chaplais, Christian: "What Augmented Reality Can Bring to the
Industry and Why it Will Take Time", 2016,
http://www.apriso.com/blog/2016/11/what-augmented-
reality-can-bring-to-the-industry-and-why-it-will-take-
time/

Clausen, Elke: "Digitale Transformation - So revolutionieren Sie
Ihre Leadgenerierung: Auf Messeerfolg programmiert",
2016

Conrad, Saskia: "Mobile Applikationen im Tourismus", 2013

Court, David et al.: "The consumer decision journey",
http://www.mckinsey.com/business-functions/marketing-
and-sales/our-insights/the-consumer-decision-journey

Czarnetzki, Stefan: "Allgemeine Akzeptanz von Servicerobotern", 2016

D

Dettweiler, Marco: "Google sagt Allo zu Apple", 2016, http://www.faz.net/aktuell/technik-motor/computer-internet/neuer-messenger-ausprobiert-google-sagt-allo-zu-apple-14444681.html

Dörner, Ralf et al. (ed.): "Virtual und Augmented Reality (VR/AR)", 2013

Dolcourt, Jessica: "This truly is a handy phone", 2016, https://www.cnet.com/news/handy-phone-gives-travelers-free-data/

Douag, Sarah: "Erste humanoide Roboter an der Rezeption" in: Hospitality Inside Special Expo Real, 2015

E

Eichborn, Marcus: "Kundenzufriedenheit verbessern: Beispiel Digital Signage in Hotels", 2015,

http://www.videro.com/magazin/trends-
news/kundenzufriedenheit-verbessern-beispiel-digital-
signage-hotels

Eickmeier, Frank: "Beacons & Datenschutz: Eine rechtliche
Einordnung" in: eCommerce Magazine 01/2015

Esch, Franz-Rudolf (ed.): „Moderne Markenführung", 2005

Esch, Franz-Rudolf / Brunner, Christian / Hartmann, Kerstin:
"Kaufprozessorientierte Modelle der Markenführung auf
dem Prüfstand: Ein Vergleich mit einem ganzheitlichen,
verhaltenswissenschaftlichen Model der Markenführung",
2008

Esch, Franz-Rudolf / Langner, Tobias: "Branding als
Grundlage zum Markenaufbau" in: Esch, Franz-Rudolf
(ed.): "Moderne Markenführung", 2005

Esch, Franz-Rudolf / Knörle, Christian: "Omni-Channel-
Strategien durch Customer-Touchpoint-Management
erfolgreich realisieren" in: Binckenbanck, Lars / Elste,
Rainer (ed.): "Digitalisierung im Vertrieb – Strategien
zum Einsatz neuer Technologien in
Vertriebsorganisationen", 2016

Eugster, Jörg et al.: "Die ganze Welt des Online-Marketings",
2015

F

Fedossov, Alexander: "Was sind Chatbots und wo sind ihre Grenzen?", 2016, https://wollmilchsau.de/personalmarketing/wer-oder-was-sind-chatbots/

Fischer, Peter: "Digital Signage – Werbliche Kommunikation am Point of Sale auf Flachbildschirmen. Theoretische Hintergründe, Aufgaben und Wirkungsmessungen.", 2010

Frey, Carl Benedikt / Osborne, Michael A.: "The Future of Employment", 2013

Friedlander, R.J.: "Are Robots Changing the Way That Guest Experience is Measured in the Hotel Industry?", 2016, http://www.4hoteliers.com/features/article/99984hoteliers.com

Funk, Christian: "Digitalisation is key" in: CIM – Conference & Incentive Management, Special GBB, 2015

G

Gardini, Marco: "Marketing-Management in der Hotellerie", 3rd Edition, 2015

Geiger, Harley Lorenz: "A Standard for Digital Signage Privacy" in: Müller, Jörg et al.: "Pervasive Advertising", 2011

Gentile, Chiara / Spiller, Nicola / Noci, Giuliano: "How to Sustain the Customer Experience: An Overview of Experience Components that Co-create Value With the Customer" in: "European Management Journal", Issue 5, 2007

Gentsch, Peter: "Digitale Transformation im E-Business: Conversational Commerce als Game Changer", 2016, https://www.xing.com/communities/posts/digitale-transformation-im-e-business-conversational-commerce-als-game-changer-1012440284

Gertschen, Alex: "In-House-Apps für die Hotel Gäste" in: „fokus, htr hotel revue", No.17, 2013, P. 12

Glattes, Karin: "Der Konkurrenz ein Kundenerlebnis voraus: Customer Experience Management", 2016

Gruen, Keith: "Pre-assigning room numbers can lead to lost business", 2013, https://hetras.wordpress.com/tag/room-assignment/

Gründel, Verena: "Digital-Signage-Trends 2015: So erobern Interaktive den Crosschannel-Markt." in: iBusiness, 2014

Günther, Pamela: „Yield Management als Erfolgsfaktor der Hotellerie: Eine kritische Evaluation der automatisierten Yield-Management-Systeme", 2013

Graf, René / Weckesser, Peter: "Autonomous roomservice in a hotel" in: "Intelligent Autonomous Vehicles", 1998

Grzona, Lukas: "Immer den günstigsten Hotelpreis finden", 2016, https://www.netzsieger.de/k/hotelsuchmaschinen

Gielnik, Nina-Franziska: "Robots powered by IBM Watson erobern die Hotellerie: ein personalisiertes Hotelerlebnis mit Concierge Connie", 2016, https://cloudikon.de/robots-powered-by-ibm-watson-erobern-die-hotellerie/

H

Haderlein, Andreas: "Die digitale Zukunft des stationären Handels: Auf allen Kanälen zum Kunden", 2nd Edition, 2013

Halbach, Wulf: "Interfaces: medien- und kommunikationstheoretische Elemente einer Interface-Theorie", 1994

Hansa, Kira: "Dieses Personal zickt nicht rum und will kein
Trinkgeld", 2016,
https://www.welt.de/reise/deutschland/article153085621/
Dieses-Personal-zickt-nicht-rum-und-will-kein-
Trinkgeld.html

Hansmann, Karl-Werner (ed.): "Management des Wandels",
2012

Hedemann, Falk / Tißler, Jan (ed.): "Upload Magazin 21:
Virtuelle Welten", 2015

Heger, Rainer: "Entwicklung eines Systems zur interaktiven
Gestaltung und Auswertung von manuellen
Montagetätigkeiten in der virtuellen Realität.", 1998

Heilig, Morten: "The cinema of the future." in: Packer, Randall /
Jordan, Ken: "Multimedia: From Wagner to virtual
reality", 2002

Heinemann, Gerrit et al.: "Digitale Transformation oder digitale
Disruption im Handel", 2016

Heinemann, Gerrit / Gaiser, Christian: "SoLoMo – Always-on
im Handel: Die soziale, lokale und mobile Zukunft des
Omnichannel-Shopping", 3rd Edition, 2016

Hellrung, Niels et al.: "Einbettung assistierender Technologien in Gesundheitsnetzwerke" in: Leimeister, Jan Marco: "Technologiegestützte Dienstleistungsinnovation in der Gesundheitswirtschaft", 2012

Hennig, Carsten: "Tablets sind nun Rezeptionist und Concierge im Hotel der Zukunft" in: "Hotelling", 2014, https://hottelling.net/2014/10/20/tablets-sind-nun-rezeptionist-und-concierge-im-hotel-der-zukunft-hetras-und-suitepad-starten-pilotprojekt-im-new-generation-hotel-ruby-sofie-vienna/

Herbstritt, Kathrin: "Customer Experience Management: Konzept eines entscheidungsorientierten Managementansatzes im B2B-Dienstleistungsbereich", 2015

Higley, Jeff / Minerd, Nick: "US hotel performance for total-year 2016, Q4 2016", 2017, http://www.hotelnewsnow.com/Articles/108067/STR-US-hotel-performance-for-total-ycar-2016-Q4-2016

Hirt, Michaela / Monard, Frédéric: "Customer Experience Management (CEM) – Kundenerlebnisse aktiv gestalten und steuern", 2013

Hoffmeister, Christian: "Digitale Geschäftsmodelle richtig einschätzen", 2013

Hucho, Michael: "Alles digital? Über die Digitalisierung in Hotellerie und Gastronomie" in: "Hoga aktiv", 2016

Hütz, Stefanie: "Erst der Content, sonst kein Vergnügen" in: Stores+Shops Extra Digital Signage Trends No. 6, 2014

I

IBM Institute for Business Value: "Digital Transformation Creating New Business Models Where Digital Meets Physical", 2011

J

Jackson, John: "Using a chatbot to start a conversation with restaurant regulars", 2016, http://venturebeat.com/2016/10/06/using-a-chatbot-to-start-a-conversation-with-restaurant-regulars/

Jaffe, Joseph: "Flip the Funnel: How to Use Existing Customers to Gain New Ones", 2010

Jaser, Michael: "Evaluation, Bewertung und Implementierung verschiedener Cross-Plattform Development Ansätze für

Mobile Internet Devices auf Basis von Web-
Technologien", 2011

Jensen, Torsten / Wille, Sebastian / Wehn, Norbert:
"Multisensorische Event-Erlebnisse auf Basis der
iBeacon-Technologie – Bericht aus der Praxis" in: Zanger,
Cornelia: "Events und Emotionen", 2015

Jones, Michael Forrest: "How do hotels assign rooms to
guests?", 2012, https://www.quora.com/How-do-hotels-
assign-rooms-to-guests

K

Kamps, Ingo: "Einstieg in erfolgreiches Mobile Marketing",
2015

Kauer-Berk, Oliver: "Größter Schwachpunkt ist fehlende
Vergleichbarkeit", 2016,
https://www.welt.de/reise/article152553504/Groesster-
Schwachpunkt-ist-fehlende-Vergleichbarkeit.html

Kaufmann, Alexander: "Beacons: Vom Piloten zum
Erfolgsprojekt" in: e-Commerce Magazine, 2015,
http://www.e-commerce-magazin.de/fachartikel/beacons-
vom-piloten-zum-erfolgsprojekt

Kaup, Michael: "Chancen und Risiken von Digital Signage", 2010

Kasavana, Michael / Brooks, Richard: "Managing Front Office Operations", 8th Edition, 2009

Kastin, Troy: "5 ways iBeacons could make a splash in the Event Industry", 2016, http://blog.attendease.com/blog/5-ways-ibeacons-could-make-a-splash-in-the-event-industry

Kelsen, Keith: "Unleashing The Power Of Digital Signage", 2010

Kleingers, Sarah: "Was kostet die virtuelle Welt", 2016, https://recordbay.de/virtual-reality-kosten/

Klingler-Deiseroth, Carmen: "Serviceroboter gewinnen an Marktreife", 2014, http://www.vdi-nachrichten.com/Technik-Wirtschaft/Serviceroboter-gewinnen-an-Marktreife

Kolasinski, Eugenia: "Simulator Sickness in Virtual Environments", 1995

Kotowski, Timo: "Einchecken ohne Hotelrezeption", 2015, http://www.faz.net/aktuell/wirtschaft/conichi-will-die-hotelrezeption-abloesen-13794028.html

Kroeber-Riel, Werner / Weinberg, Peter / Gröppel-Klein, Andrea: "Konsumentenverhalten", 2009

Kroeber-Riel, Werner / Gröppel-Klein, Andrea: "Konsumentenverhalten", 10th Edition, 2013

Kühl, Eike: "Auf dem Heimtrainer durchs schwarze Loch", 2016, http://www.zeit.de/digital/internet/2016-08/virtual-reality-fitness-radfahren-google-street-view

Kühl, Eicke: "Hey, du Mensch!", 2016, http://www.zeit.de/digital/internet/2016-04/facebook-messenger-chatbots-zukunft

Kumar, V. and Shah, D.: "Building and sustaining profitable customer loyalty for the 21st century" in: Journal of Retailing, 80(4), 2004, P. 317–329

Kunz, Christian: "Fast 60 Prozent der Suchanfragen stammen von Mobilgeräten", 2016, https://www.seo-suedwest.de/1834-report-60-prozent-suchanfragen-mobilgeraete.html

Kwidzinski, Raphaela: "Die großen Portale haben ihre Tücken" in: Allgemeine Hotel- und Gastronomie-Zeitung, No. 50, 2012

L

Leimeister, Jan Marco: "Technologiegestützte Dienstleistungsinnovation in der Gesundheitswirtschaft", 2012

Leinenbach, Stefan: "Interaktive Geschäftsmodellierung: Dokumentation von Prozesswissen in einer Virtual Reality-gestützten Unternehmungsvisualisierung", 2000

Levy, Karyne: "The Concierge At This Fancy San Francisco Hotel Uses Google Glass", 2014, http://www.businessinsider.com/the-concierge-at-this-fancy-san-francisco-hotel-uses-google-glass-2014-4?IR=T

Licht, Lucas: "Augmented and Mixed Reality – Die Welt als Hyperlink", 2010

Ling, Isabel: "Cornell Robotics Startup Revolutionizes Hospitality" in: The Cornell Daily, 2016, http://cornellsun.com/2016/01/29/c-u-robotics-startup-revolutionizes-hospitality/

Linnhoff-Popien, Claudia / Zaddach, Michael / Grahl, Andreas: "Marktplätze im Umbruch – Digitale Strategien für Services im Mobilen Internet", 2015

Lobe, Adrian: "Allo, wer spricht denn da?", 2016,
http://www.faz.net/aktuell/feuilleton/medien/neue-google-
app-allo-wer-spricht-denn-da-14446431.html

Lobe, Adrian: "Die Welt durch die Brille der Softwarekonzerne",
2014, http://www.tagesspiegel.de/medien/augmented-
reality-die-welt-durch-die-brille-der-
softwarekonzerne/11114582.html

M

Madary, Michael / Metzinger, Thomas: "Real Virtuality: A
Code of Ethical Conduct. Recommendations for Good
Scientific Practice and the Consumers of VR-
Technology", 2016,
http://journal.frontiersin.org/article/10.3389/frobt.2016.00
003/full

Mahnicke, Rüdiger: "Business Travel Management: Praxis-
Know-How für den Einkäufer", 2013

Maire, Ludovic: "Conversational commerce is about to
revolutionize retail", 2016,
https://www.valtech.com/blog/conversational-commerce-
is-about-to-revolutionize-retail/

Mallik, Neha: "How Hotels can use Beacons to Enhance Guest Experiences", 2014, http://blog.beaconstac.com/2014/07/how-hotels-can-use-beacons-to-enhance-guest-experiences/

Mandelbaum, Abi: "How hotels could use augmented reality", 2015, https://ehotelier.com/insights/2015/07/21/how-hotels-could-use-augmented-reality/

May, Kevin: "Expedia spent \$2.8 billion on marketing in 2014", 2014, https://www.tnooz.com/article/expedia-marketing-technology-spend-2014/

Mayer-Vorfelder, Matthias: "Kundenerfahrung im Dienstleistungsprozess: Eine theoretische und empirische Analyse", 2011

McGee, Matt: "Social Media Via Google Glass: Florida Agency Has An App For That", 2014, http://marketingland.com/social-media-via-google-glass-florida-agency-app-78218

Mehler-Bicher, Anett / Steiger, Lothar: "Augmented Reality: Theorie und Praxis", 2nd Edition, 2014

Melzer, Michael: "Tipps und Tricks für den Rezeptionisten: Organisiertes Arbeiten am Hotelempfang", 2014

Milgram, Paul et al.: "Augmented Reality: A class of displays on the reality-virtuality continuum" in: SPIE: "Telemanipulator and Telepresence Technologies", Journal 2351, 1994

Müller, Andreas: "Oculus Rift & Datenschutz: Diese Daten sammelt die VR-Brille", 2016, https://www.turn-on.de/play/ratgeber/oculus-rift-datenschutz-diese-daten-sammelt-die-vr-brille-76739

Müller, Jörg et al.: "Pervasive Advertising", 2011

Müller, Mirjam: "Augmented Reality in der Praxis", 2011, http://heftarchiv.internetworld.de/2011/Ausgabe-21-2011/Augmented-Reality-in-der-Praxis

N

Noël, Jean-Marc / Pohle, Jan: "Vertrauen in E-Commerce", 2005

O

O'Conner, Peter: "Using Computers in Hospitality", 3rd Edition, 2004

O'Neill, Sean: "Choose your own room, for a fee", 2011, http://www.budgettravel.com/blog/hotels-choose-your-own-room-for-a-fee,11698/

O'Meara, Lenore: "Hotels struggle to manage electronic communications" in: Hospitality Technology No. 14, 2010

P

Packer, Randall / Jordan, Ken: "Multimedia: From Wagner to Virtual Reality", 2002

Plass-Fleßenkämper, Benedikt: "In dieser Küche steht ein Roboter hinterm Herd", 2015, https://www.wired.de/collection/tech/moley-robotics-erfindet-den-vollautomatischen-koch

Plewinski, Tina: "Amazon will Kunden mit hochwertigen Inspirationen verführen", 2016, https://www.amazon-watchblog.de/sortiment/626-amazon-hochwertige-inspirationen-verfuehren.html

216

Pluta, Werner: "Heute kocht der Roboter", 2015,
http://www.golem.de/news/moley-robotics-der-roboter-
bereitet-das-essen-zu-1504-113511.html

Pose, Ronald / Regan, Matthew: "Techniques for Reducing
Virtual Reality Latency with Architectural Support and
Consideration of Human Factors" in: Brusilovski, Peter /
Kommers, Piet: "Multimedia, Hypermedia and Virtual
Reality", 1994

Q

Qattawi, Lisa: "Barrieren im Wissensmanagement", 2006

R

Radde, Björn: "Virtual und Augmented Reality", 2014,
http://www.page-consulting.de/allgemein/virtual-und-
augmented-reality/

Ray, Nilanjan: "Emerging Innovative Marketing Strategies in the
Tourism Industry", 2015

Ravikumar, Rajath: "Why hotels should adopt beacon technology before it's too late", 2016, http://digitalhub.mindtree.com/why-hotels-should-adopt-beacon-technology-before-its-too-late/

Recke, Tobias / Einhorn, Marting: "Markencontrolling bei der Dr. Ing. h.c. Porsche AG" in: Burmann, Christoph / König, Verena / Meurer, Jörg (ed.): "Identitätsbasierte Luxusmarkenführung", 2012

Reil, Harald: "iBeacon – Apples neues Ortungssystem könnte dem stationären Handel wieder auf die Sprünge helfen" in: GENIOS WirtschaftsWissen No. 11, 2014

Richters, Kim: "Wie ein Berliner Startup den Hotelaufenthalt digitalisieren will", 2016, http://www.gruenderszene.de/allgemein/conichi-launch-finanzierung

Rotberg, Florian: "Digital Signage-Markt 2010", 2010

S

Sauter, Werner / Scholz, Christina: "Kompetenzorientiertes Wissensmanagement: Gesteigerte Performance mit dem Erfahrungswissen aller Mitarbeiter", 2015

Sinclair, Jeff: "Proven Ways of Using Beacons to Redefine the Event Experience", 2015, http://www.eventmanagerblog.com/using-beacons-event-experience

Schaeffler, Jimmy: "Digital Signage: Software, Networks, Advertising, and Displays. A Primer for Understanding the Business", 2013

Schallmo, Daniel: "Jetzt digital transformieren: So gelingt die erfolgreiche Digitale Transformation Ihres Geschäftsmodells", 2016

Schilling, Karolina: "Apps machen", 2016

Schmidl, Christian: "Neue Technologien in der mobilen Kundenansprache am Flughafen München" in: Linnhoff-Popien, Claudia / Zaddach, Michael / Grahl, Andreas: "Markplätze im Umbruch – Digitale Strategien für Services im Mobilen Internet", 2015

Schmidt, Holger: "Menschen vertrauen Robotern oft blind", 2016, https://netzoekonom.de/2016/11/15/12236/

Schmitt, Bernd: "Customer Experience Management: A Revolutionary Approach To Connecting With Your Customers", 2003

Schnitzlein, Maximilian: "Grundlagen des Digital Signage", 2015, P. 3

Schorer, Matthias: "Ubiquitous Computing ist Realität", 2016, http://www.computerwoche.de/a/ubiquitous-computing-ist-realitaet,3093580

Schraft, Rolf-Dieter / Volz, Hansjörg: "Serviceroboter: Innovative Technik in Dienstleistung und Versorgung", 1996

Schüffler, Christine: "Supply Management in der Hotelbrache. Grundlagen, Erfolgsfaktoren und Gestaltungsempfehlungen", 2008

Schüller, Anne: "Touch. Point. Sieg. Kommunikation in Zeiten der digitalen Transformation", 2016

Schulz, Axel: "eTourismus: Prozesse und Systeme: Informationsmanagement im Tourismus", 2nd Edition, 2015

Schulz, Axel / Weithörner, Uwe / Goecke, Robert: "Informationssystem im Tourismus", 2010

Sheff, David / Eddy, Andy: "Game Over: How Nintendo Conquered the World", 1999

Smith, Shaun / Wheeler, Joe: "Managing the Customer Experience: Turning Customers into Advocates", 2002

Sölter, Marc: "Hotelvertrieb, Yield-Management und Dynamic Pricing in der Hotellerie", 2007

Stauss, Bernd / Seidel, Wolfgang: „Beschwerdemanagement: Unzufriedene Kunden als profitable Zielgruppe", 5th Edition, 2014

Stampfl, Nora: "Die Zukunft der Dienstleistungsökonomie: Momentaufnahme und Perspektiven", 2011

Statista: "Online Reisebuchungen" https://de.statista.com/outlook/262/137/online-reisebuchungen/deutschland#, 2015

SuitePad GmbH press release, 2013, http://www.suitepad.de/wp-content/uploads/2013/10/Service-that-sells-Wie-Concierge-Tablets-zu-mehr-Zusatzverk%C3%A4ufen-im-Hotel-f%C3%BChren.pdf

T

Telschow, Stephan: "Digital Signage – die
Kommunikationsrevolution am Point Of Sale" in:
Gesellschaft für Innovative Marktforschung Update 1,
2010

Telschow, Stephan: "Im Dialog mit dem Shopper" in:
Markenartikel No. 6, 2010

Tezlaff, Jutta: "Digital Signage schafft neue Möglichkeiten für
die Markenkommunikation am Point of Sale" in: "Marke
41" No. 5, 2008

The Futures Company for InterContinental Hotel: "Creating
'moments of trust' The key to building successful brand
relationships in the Kinship Economy", 2013

The International Federation Of Robotics: "World-Robotics-
Studie: Service-Roboter erobern die Welt", 2015,
http://www.presseportal.de/pm/115415/3135305

Tißler, Jan: "Google Cardboard Anleitung: Virtual Reality zum
Taschengeldpreis" in: Hedemann, Falk / Tißler, Jan (ed.):
"Upload Magazine 21: Virtuelle Welten", 2015

Toedt, Michael: "Beacons – Top or Flop for the Hospitality
Industry?", 2015,
http://www.hospitalitynet.org/news/4073267.html

Tönnis, Marcus: "Augmented Reality – Einblicke in die
Erweiterte Realität", 2010

Trunkfield, David / Mayer, Nicolas: "Standing out from
the crowd: European cities hotel forecast for 2017 and
2018", 2017, http://www.pwc.com/gx/en/hospitality-
leisure/assets/european-hotels-forecast-report-2017-2018-
web.pdf

U

Urbach, Niels / Ahlemann, Frederik: "IT-Management im
Zeitalter der Digitalisierung", 2016

V

Voigt, Kai-Ingo: "Kulturbewußtes Management – Wandel von
Unternehmensstrategie und Unternehmenskultur", in:
Hansmann, Karl-Werner (ed.): "Management des
Wandels", 2012, P. 55-77

W

Wächter, Mark: "Mobile Strategy", 2016

Waldmax, Max: "Why 2016 needs to be the year of the digital guest standard", 2016, https://www.tnooz.com/article/hotel-guest-experience-digital-standard/

Warnecke, Tobias: "Hotelmarkt Deutschland 2016", 2016

Warnholtz, Anna: "Und, gut geschlafen?", 2007, https://www.welt.de/reise/article785752/Und-gut-geschlafen.html

Watkinson, Matt: "The Ten Principles Behind Great Customer Experience", 2013

Weissmann, Saya: "5 Hotel Brands With Useful Mobile Apps", 2013, http://digiday.com/brands/5-hotel-brands-with-useful-mobile-apps/

Weller, Manuel: "Worauf Sie im Hotel achten sollten", 2015, http://biztravel.fvw.de/reisesicherheit-worauf-sie-im-hotel-achten-sollten/1/142953/4081

Wider, Martin: "Mobile Disruption – oder warum der richtige Einsatz von Mobile für den Einzelhandel überlebenswichtig ist." in: Heinemann, Gerrit et al.: "Digitale Transformation oder digitale Disruption im Handel", 2016

Wilkens, Andreas: "Datenschutzbeauftrage Voßhoff warnt vor Amazon Echo", 2016, https://www.heise.de/newsticker/meldung/Datenschutzbea uftragte-Vosshoff-warnt-vor-Amazon-Echo-3380364.html

Wolf, Isabella: "Augmented Reality am Point of Sale", 2016, http://www.marketmentor.org/de/augmented-reality-point-sale/

Wolf, John: "Apple Pay Checks In to Marriott – First Hotel Company to Offer the Service to Its Guests", 2015, http://news.marriott.com/2015/03/apple-pay-checks-in-to-marriott-first-hotel-company-to-offer-the-service-to-its-guests/

Wray, Evan: "5 Dinge, die Unternehmen über Chatbots wissen sollten" in: InternetWorld Business, 2016, http://www.internetworld.de/technik/bots/5-dinge-unternehmen-chatbots-wissen-1134601.html

X

Xiang, Zheng / Thssyadiah, Iis (ed.): "Information and Communication Technologies in Tourism 2014", 2014

Y

Yackey, Bill: "Digital Signage in the Hotel Industry", 2012

Z

Zanger, Cornelia: "Events und Emotionen", 2015

Ziefle, Martina: "Ungewissheit und Unsicherheit bei der Einführung neuer Technologien"

List of figures

List of image sources

Fig. 1:   own diagram

Fig. 2:   http://www.trendsderzukunft.de/japaner-plant-
            hotel-mit-roboter-als-angestellte/2015/01/28/

Fig. 3:   http://bilder1.n-
            tv.de/img/incoming/origs13878796/ 95827396-
            w1000-h960/imago-st-103009350012-
            61662371.jpg

Fig. 4:   http://www.digitaltrends.com/home/moley-
            robotics-introduces-robot-chef-that-makes-high-
            quality-food/

Fig. 5:   https://www.densorobotics-
            europe.com/sites/default/files/image/CaseStudies/
            Robofox/rofobox_de_15_Large700x466.jpg

Fig. 6:   http://www.isignage.io/hospitality/

Fig. 7:   https://hottelling.files.wordpress.com/2015/05/
            suitepad-tablet-pc.jpg

Fig. 8:   http://www.etbtravelnews.com/wp-
            content/uploads/2016/02/Park-Hotel-Hong-
            Kong_Handy-phone_LR.jpg

228

Fig. 9:   https://www.beaconwinkel.nl/wp-
               content/uploads/2015/08/Kontakt.io-smart-
               beacon.jpg

Fig. 10:   https://s.aolcdn.com/hss/storage/midas/
               4f2c920c9bcd84a16c4346a26a6ce6bd/202661688
               /BS4A0123.JPG

Fig. 11:   http://www.drhu.eu/wp-
               content/uploads/2012/05/Order-of-reality-
               concepts.png

Fig. 12:   http://www.augmentedrealitytrends.com/wp-
               content/uploads/2014/09/Augmented-Reality.jpg

Fig. 13:   http://marketingland.com/wp-content/ml-
               loads/2014/03/google-glass-b2-hotel.jpg

Fig. 14:   http://www.staywyse.org/wp-
               content/uploads/sites/4/2014/05/screen-shot-2013-
               03-07-at-9-40-47-pm.png?w=150

Fig. 15:   http://foodpix.co/wp-
               content/uploads/2016/08/Foodpix-Augmented-
               reality-food-01-1024x680.jpg

Fig. 16:   http://bilder1.n-
                tv.de/img/incoming/origs18981436/ 3782737124-
                w1000-h960/Amazon-Echo-schwarz.jpg

Fig. 17:   http://www.neorcha.com/wp-
                content/uploads/2016/07/beacons.jpeg

Fig. 18:   http://www.iris.net/platform/plugins/

Cover: Canva.com

Photo author: Swetlana Ermisch

List of abbreviations

Anon.	Anonymous
AIM	AOL Instant Messenger
AOL	America OnLine
API	Application Programming Interface
App	Application
AR	Augmented Reality
ARPU	Average Revenue Per User
B2B	Business-to-Business
B2C	Business-to-Consumer
BDSG	Bundesdatenschutzgesetz (Federal Data Protection Act)
BetrVG	Betriebsverfassungsgesetzt (German Works Constitution Act)
ca.	circa
CEM	Customer Experience Management
CEO	Chief Operating Officer
CDO	Chief Digital Officer
CMO	Chief Marketing Officer
CMS	Content Management System
CRM	Customer Relationship Management
CRS	Central Reservation System
CSS	Cascading Style Sheets
eBusiness	Electronic Business
eCommerce	Electronic Commerce
eDistribution	Electronic Distribution
DIY	Do It Yourself
Ed.	Editor

E-Mail	Electronic Mail
et al.	et alii (and others)
e.g.	exempli gratia (for example)
f.	following (page)
ff.	and following (pages)
Fig.	Figure
GPS	Global Positioning System
HTTP	Hyper Text Transfer Protocol
HTML	Hyper Text Markup Language
i.e.	id est (that is)
Inc.	Incorporation
IT	Information Technology
iOS	iPhone Operating System
IoT	Internet of Things
LAN	Local Area Network
LED	Light Emitting Diode
Max.	maximal
No.	Number
ooH	out of Home
OTA	Online Travel Agency
P.	Page
PC	Personal Computer
PCI	Payment Card Industry
PMS	Property Management System
QR-Code	Quick Response Code
RevPar	Revenue Per Available Room
RFID	Radio Frequency Identification
RMS	Revenue Management System
ROI	Return on Investment

SEA	Search Engine Advertising
SEM	Search Engine Marketing
SEO	Search Engine Optimization
TMG	Telemediengesetz (German Telemedia Act)
TV	Television
VIP	Very Important Person
VR	Virtual Reality
Wi-Fi	Wireless Fidelity
WLAN	Wireless Local Area Network
WML	Wireless Markup Language

Index